SHIPS

A Pictorial History
from Noah's *Ark* to the U.S.S. *United States*

PUBLISHER'S NOTE

You are about to enjoy the most comprehensive visual record of the history of ships ever assembled in one single volume. Edited by an acknowledged authority, it takes you from the very beginnings up to the late 1950's when presumably we all became aware of the subject from personal observation and experience. Here are those rich, formative years before our own age of awareness, displayed pictorially (over 400 photos) and accompanied by a knowledgeable and pertinent commentary so that we might enjoy its reading over and over again. The British editor may have tended to emphasise the European contribution, but since his expertise in the field is unassailable and since the wealth of detail he has provided is as impressive as in any other published document within our memory, we hope you agree that a small bias is more than compensated for by such a massive compendium of information and entertainment.

Other Pictorial Histories in this Series
Each containing 400-650 illustrations:

MOTORING
A Pictorial History of the First 150 Years
by L. T. C. ROLT

FLIGHT
A Pictorial History from the Wright Brothers to Supersonic
by JOHN W. R. TAYLOR

RAILWAYS
A Pictorial History of the First 150 Years
by C. HAMILTON ELLIS

First Published in this Edition, 1974, by
Peebles Press International Inc.,
140 Riverside Drive, New York, N.Y. 10024

Originally Published by Hulton Press Ltd., London, as
A PICTURE HISTORY OF SHIPS

ISBN 0 85690 007 9

Printed and bound in Gt. Britain by
Redwood Burn Ltd., Trowbridge & Esher.

The United States Frigate *Constellation*, the oldest American fighting ship in existance now berthed at Baltimore. From an original painting by Roy Cross (by permission of the Malcolm Henderson Gallery, London).

SHIPS

A Pictorial History from
Noah's *Ark* to the U.S.S. *United States*

by
C. HAMILTON ELLIS

PEEBLES PRESS
New York: London

Foreword to this Edition

What is a ship?

It is a vessel that can be propelled and navigated across the Seven Seas, or, in our own time, under them or even under the polar ice. In America, an aircraft, or a space craft, is often called a ship. But those might just as well be called vehicles, with the exception of the airship (which is extremely rare nowadays). That is indeed a vessel, unlike a train, an automobile or, if you like, an ox-cart. Not even a hovercraft is a vessel, when we look at recent developments in seagoing, for while at sea it is still a vehicle, sustained on the water by mechanical means and production of pressure to that end. It becomes a vessel only if its engines break down and oblige it to float, rather as an exhausted swimmer may yet float until help (one hopes) may arrive. So this is a chronicle of ships and while some incidental airships occur, they need not be disqualified.

Another rhetorical question. What linked the human penetrations of our ancient and long-suffering planet? Such penetration was made, initially, on two flat feet belonging to each person; then by the taming and training of the horse, with four much stronger feet, and then by the navigable vessel which alone could link separate continents in the early history of mankind. Therein began sea-lore, with the use of the vessel and the knowledge of navigation.

Navigation, indeed, is older than mankind, for at a remote time long before man's recorded migrations, migratory birds and sea-beasts knew all about it, by means mysterious to us. Amongst much else, Masefield was to write:

> *I must go down to the sea again,*
> *To the roving Gypsy life;*
> *To the gull's way, and the whale's way,*
> *And a wind like a whetted knife.*

The Editor of this book never claimed to be a sailor. At an early age he took the helm of a sailing craft (under a kindly eye), and years later he knew the inside of a ship's galley. But his approach is ever that of the student, in the best sense of that much-abused term. When the Festival of Britain arrived in 1951, he had been entrusted with the theme-writing for the Marine Sections, and was glad when his brave—and by then frail—King George VI liked them and said so publicly.

But for the ship, America as we know it might never have happened. Yet Thor Heyerdahl has shown, practically, that the Atlantic could be crossed by a primitive Egyptian papyrus ship. He showed that the Polynesians may have come from South America, by taking his own party from Peru to islands south of the Marquesas on a balsa wood raft, using the Humboldt Current and one square sail bearing the mask of the great god Kon-Tiki.

Who shall say what did, or did not, happen in distant time through the agency of The Ship?

Introduction

HUMAN history is founded on the wish to survive. The wish to survive is implemented by trade, and trade cannot exist without transport. No man knows when one of our species first used a pack animal. No man knows who invented the wheel. No man knows who first made a boat, or something that would float and be at least crudely navigable, but he was probably Eastern. The floating log evolved to the catamaran, and that to the dug-out canoe. When there were no trees, the first boat was a sort of basket. Once man could navigate, great migrations became possible.

At a remote time, cosmic calamity caused annihilating floods, and even then the large vessel could be used to preserve man and beast. The Flood occurs in legend all over the world. Most circumstantial is the Middle Eastern story of Noah. Opinion, learned and otherwise, is much divided on Noah's Ark—whether she contained the equivalent of a large menagerie-farm and eventually stranded on a Mesopotamian hillock, or whether she carried the entire animal creation and ultimately ran aground on Mount Ararat. But if, as recorded in the Book of Genesis, she was a three-decker, 450 ft. long, 75 ft. in the beam and 45 ft. deep, she was quite a ship.

The Ship in the Ancient World

Well over 1,500 years before the Biblical date of Noah's flood there was the papyrus canoe. It was not properly a vessel; the water came in and the craft floated through the buoyancy of the reeds composing it. The ancient navigator of the Nile had no particular objection to getting wet. But somewhere in the Middle East, possibly during the fourth millennium B.C., emerged the practice of pitching the basketwork boat with bitumen and thus making it watertight.

In the Egyptian Old Kingdom, which ended about 2,745 B.C., the relatively large wooden boat had already appeared. Built of short acacia planks, it was propelled by oarsmen in two double rows, it had a single sail, and the very shallow hull was about 60 ft. long by 11 ft. wide. Steering was by large oars astern. To prevent the shallow, flimsy hull from hogging, a long rope truss was carried longitudinally on kingposts, and passed under bow and stern. The principle may still be seen on some river craft. One of the longest "runs" in the ancient Egyptian shipping world was that down the Red Sea and beyond to the rich region called Punt. Just where Punt was, is unknown, but an African location seems probable. The explorer Herkhuf brought back a pygmy.

By the time of the formidable Queen Hatshepsut (fifteenth century B.C.), great advances had been made in the rig; there was a single mast amidships with yards nearly as long as the vessel itself, each yard consisting of a pair of spars spliced together at the mast, the lower pair keeping the sail taut. The halyards were led aft, and in the stern also were two enormous steering oars with downward curving tillers.

Thus in the ships of the Pharaohs do we see the birth of the seagoing sailing ship, and also of the galley, and the galley was to be the characteristic Mediterranean ship through many succeeding centuries, not finally to vanish until the beginning of the nineteenth century. Its latter-day reputation was most unsavoury; we retain a picture of a beautiful craft, moving like a sentient thing with the lovely rhythm of her oars, and then as she goes to windward our other senses catch the stench, and the crack of the lash on the bare backs of the chained oarsmen.

Of the earliest ships belonging to the Minoan civilization of Crete, little can be learnt. Main power was by oars; the single square sail was auxiliary. Even in Homeric times the bireme, with a double bank of oars, had arrived, and so, by the time of Pericles, had the trireme. The backbone of the galley, as of succeeding ships, was the keel.

To this day, there is no finer description of an ancient navy putting to sea than that in Thucydides' *History of the Peloponnesian War* at the end of the fourth century B.C., when Athens endeavoured to conquer Syracuse. No slaves were at the oars; the men rowed with enthusiasm, as seamen, and in the same account is a record of 168 miles being covered in a day and a night, a remarkable achievement.

Greek merchant ships could be markedly different from the warships. Speed was of less account and capacity of much more. The warship had much in common with the Levantine ship, generally called Phoenician, which likewise might have two banks of oars, and which was sufficiently seaworthy to voyage far out beyond the Pillars of Hercules to the Tin Islands, as the British Isles were called.

The earliest recorded Greek merchantmen were sailing ships proper. In later designs, oars reappeared, but sail was chiefly relied on. The hull was built up of pine planks, but the keel was stoutly built of oak, it being customary to haul the ships up ashore at night and between voyages. The timber was cut and worked green, it being more pliable, and in consequence the life of a ship was short. At the same time, construction could be extraordinarily rapid. There were repeated instances of this with the fleets of Imperial Rome; 220 new ships were built in three months after a naval disaster in 256 B.C., to give but one example. This was a very early anticipation of the performance of U.S. shipyards in two world wars.

Roman ships are comparatively familiar to us owing to their occurrence in monumental reliefs, and these, in general, are accurate. From Greece, Rome inherited the war-galley, with several banks of oars, but with two relatively small masts, square-rigged, instead of the characteristic Greek single mast and sail. There would be a high forecastle and a higher poop, containing quarters for officers and other superior persons. In the larger vessels, artillery of the catapult type was mounted, and a boarding gangway (*corvus*) which had a spike at the end and was let down with a bang on the enemy's deck when coming alongside. The ram was a powerful offensive weapon (revived centuries after, in the early days of steam-driven warships).

Again different were the larger Roman merchantmen, such as those used for conveyance of corn from Egypt to Italy. In important features they anticipated the larger ships of the late Middle Ages; there was a stout stem, connected through a strong keel to the sternpost, and the hull was strengthened by long wales above the waterline. There was a big mast with a square sail, strongly braced to the stem and the stern quarter, with adequate shrouds each side, all set up by deadeyes in singularly "modern" style. Forward was a form of bowsprit carrying a spritsail or a square foresail, and by the use of the spritsail a ship was enabled to sail in a beam wind at least, and possibly in a wind a little forward of the beam. In these respects the Roman merchantman was well in advance of ships built for centuries after.

In the exuberant days of Rome—the beginning of the Decline—appeared what today we should call the luxury-galley, sumptuously appointed, overloaded with ornament, of which Caligula's pleasure craft on Lake Nemi are best known. The first of these to be recovered (fig. 14) was about 200 ft. long and 60 ft. in the beam, more of a huge palatial houseboat than a ship, perhaps most correctly described as an imperial barge. But the Mediterranean, like the Atlantic centuries later, had not only its grain-ships but its high-priced passenger packets, the liners of the period.

Let us turn northwards now. The Norse ship circumnavigated the European seaboard, it brought to Celtic Britain the full fierce impact of Nordic conquest, it brought Scandinavian adventurers through Eastern Europe into Central Asia; it crossed the Atlantic with Lief Ericsson, and between the two it brought the English to England. Though an American empire was not founded by the Vikings, certainly a Russian one was sliced out of what was then the Near East, as the yellow-haired invaders, having built new ships far inland, ravaged their way down the Volga to the Caspian.

Most fortunately, Norse ships have, in one form or another, survived the centuries and we know exactly what they were like. Further, the small boat of Norwegian fjord and mountain tarn, in its form of construction, is small sister to the Viking ship of history. The ship was double-ended, and an ancient Danish example (the Nydam boat, c. A.D. 400) was about 76 ft. long, built of oak with clinched (overlapping) planks. The Mediterranean ship was carvel-built, i.e. with the planks set edge-to-edge. The Nydam boat had a marked sheer; the stem- and stern-posts were high, the width amidships about 10½ ft., the midship section followed a shallow curve with a small keel. The hull was about 4 ft. deep amidships. Propulsion was by twenty-eight oars without, apparently, any sail. There was a single steering oar.

Two wonderfully preserved Norse vessels of the ninth century A.D. are those known as the Gokstad Ship and the Oseberg Ship, both long ships and both discovered in Norway. The former is a classic example of the long ship at its best, very strongly clincher-built of oak, 79 ft. long, nearly 17 ft. wide and just under 7 ft. deep amidships, with a deep keel. Propulsion was by thirty-two oars and a single square sail. The long-ship was a war craft, capable of making its way deep inland on harrying expeditions. It was also a ceremonial ship—the second of the surviving ninth-century Norse vessels, the Oseberg ship, carries much elaborate carving, indeed decoration was usually emphatic, often with some ferocious bird's or beast's head as figurehead.

Very long voyages were made in the *hafskib*, of the same genus, but of more robust design, proportionately shorter, drawing more water, and with a higher free-board to protect the company from heavy seas in the Atlantic and in such fierce narrow seas as those of Orkney and Shetland, and in the Minch. Of such ships was composed the first English Navy. King Edgar (959–975) placed in command one Marthusias, who combined the offices of First Sea-Lord and Admiral of the Fleet, with the finely unambiguous title of Archpirate.

Middle Ages

Northern ships of the Middle Ages remained closely akin to the Norse *hafskib*. But representations of their ships are usually crude and very misleading, suggesting a clincher-built tub. Then the ship was a favourite device on the seals of maritime towns. There was even less room for a Saxon ship on a round seal than on a crowded tapestry, and the resulting portraiture is quite as grotesque as John Leech's Victorian caricature of Harold's accident (figs. 30-31).

Oars, however, declined, decking advanced, and in the twelve hundreds appeared crude castles, fore and aft, to carry bowmen. The seal of the Cinque Port of Sandwich (1238) shows in addition a fighting top on the single mast. Towards the end of the century, the flimsy wickerwork castles had developed into substantial structures of oak. The stern rudder appears as early as 1200 in the seal of Ipswich, but steering oars are perpetuated in various later examples. A single square-rigged mast persisted. The post-Saxon ship remained a singularly comfortless craft; it is scarcely surprising that that tragic Maid of Norway, who was to have been Queen Margaret of Scots, died of seasickness and exposure. What might be called the "civilized" ship still belonged to the Mediterranean, where it impressed the English knights during the Third Crusade.

Exciting the curiosity of travelling royalty and nobility was one thing; inducing half a continent's shipwrights to change all their conventions was quite another . . . it still is! The mediaeval Mediterranean ship still had much in common with that of the ancient world, but Saracen ingenuity and influence had brought in the lateen sail, enabling the ship to sail close to the wind. It was not until the fifteenth century came in that the typical northern ship began to carry more than one mast. The Mediterranean ship had two, a mainmast and a mizzen. In the south the latter was a foremast (Arabic *mizan*, a balance, an extra, or in the argot of old New Orleans, "for lagniappe"). By the end of the century the three-master was "in", with foremast, mainmast and after-mizzen, remote forerunner of the great clippers which are still within our living memory.

The three-master of the late fifteenth century was clincher-built, very bluff in the bows. The forecastle was triangular and projected over the bows; the cabin was aft, with a clumsy poop or "summer castle" above. Our three-master of the fourteen-nineties was square-rigged, except for the lateen sail on the mizzen-mast, with sometimes a spritsail under a bowsprit forward. She was stout, sea-worthy, and by the criteria of her time reasonably manœuvrable. She was not uniformly decked; bow, waist and stern were decked at such levels as seemed convenient; the ship went up and down like the floors of an old house, with the decked cabin below the poop, and sometimes a poop royal above that. This ship made possible the long exploratory voyage, with fewer of the hazards encountered by Lief Ericsson and others in their expeditions to North America in the long-ago. Such ships were those of Columbus and the Cabots in the fourteen-nineties.

Mighty voyages of exploration were not unknown even in the ancient world. Neither the Odyssey nor the Argonaut legend can have been founded entirely on extravagant imaginings, and Herodotus mentions a Phoenician circumnavigation of Africa, out by the Red Sea, round the Cape and back by Gibraltar. But the great days of discovery began with Columbus, and went on through the succeeding centuries, with the improvement of nautical astronomy and navigational instruments. The compass is often supposed to have been China's contribution, and it was known in the East for centuries. Kipling gave an amusing description of an early English reaction to its mysteries in *Puck of Pook's Hill*. Now, in the West, men in ships began for the first time to know their planet.

Tudor to Hanover

There is no doubt about the magnitude of Henry VIII of England. He was an absolutely terrifying personage, but he founded the Royal Navy as we know it. He delighted in ships; he looked across to Spain, perhaps with mixed feelings, and knew that in tonnage was imperial greatness. In his reign, not only did the King's ships greatly increase in number and dimensions, they showed very marked advances in design, and some of these were of Mediterranean origin. The clincher-built ship declined; big ships were now carvel-built like the great Genoese ships, with much addition of cannon. The *Henri Grace à Dieu* ("Great Harry") was built in 1514 and rebuilt in 1540. In her later form she had two gun decks below the waist and remotely anticipated the "seventy-four" of the eighteenth century. The number of guns decreased as the power and efficiency of the guns grew. "Great Harry" had 186 primitive guns of several sorts when she was built. At her rebuilding, the massive muzzle-loading brass cannon, with which the nation was to refound her naval power, had come in.

The *Henri Grace à Dieu* was an early big ship of her era. Architecturally she was still in several respects mediaeval, with her forecastle projecting over the stem. Later ships lacked this projection and in its place came a beak, with the forecastle well back. It was the beginning of the galleon, with high forecastle, high poop, and flat stern pierced by ports for pursuit guns, with the cabins above. The number of decks might number four at the poop. The "Harry" was a four-master, like her forerunner the *Regent of the Tower*, and rigging became more ambitious and complex. She was square-rigged, with top-gallant masts and sails on foremast and mainmast, topsail and topgallant on her main mizzenmast, above the lateen sail, and again a topsail on the after mizzen, with lateen sail below. Henceforward, advances in rig are best described by illustration. That suffix "of the Tower", by the way, indicated a King's ship, the tower being the Tower of London. The late G. S. Laird Clowes described it as the mediaeval equivalent of "H.M.S.". The "Great Harry" was accidentally burnt in 1553.

A ship's life depended on her armament as well as her stoutness. Every ocean-going ship needed to be well armed, and this persisted through many years. While war succeeded war with the Spaniards, the Dutch and the French, not to mention encounters with pirates of all sorts, anything afloat that *did not* resemble a warship was not long for this world unless she stayed at home.

Following the death of Henry VIII, there was a slump in English prestige and a corresponding one in naval construction, but under the great Elizabeth came revival, which put England, regarded since the close of the Hundred Years War as a turbulent and schismatic minor state, back among the great European Powers. Sooner or later conclusions must be tried with the Spaniards, who, burning with fanatical religious zeal, were already giving the Flemings and Hollanders a horrible time and, still smarting over the *Affaire Catherine d'Aragon*, were determined to punish heretic England quite as severely.

Heretic England was in good mood to provoke Spain. In the West lived a fine, fierce, piratical, puritan admiral, Sir Francis Drake, who combined the pillage of

Spanish colonial ports and treasure ships with world exploration. Between 1577 and 1581 he sailed round the world in the *Pelican* (later renamed *Golden Hind*). This was no great ship; she seems to have been a bare 60 ft. from stem to stern. It is only form-room belief that when, in 1588, the vengeance of Spain was launched, the Invincible Armada's enormous galleons were assailed by what Medina-Sidonia could only regard as *small craft*. But in fact we used big ships also, as many as we could furnish, and the *small craft* notion is largely mythical. In fairness to the Spanish admiral, an embarrassed gentleman, be it recalled that he took command with the greatest reluctance he dare exhibit before King Philip—he had no pretensions to be a sailor—and that his ships were crammed with soldiers, and with priests and other monkish characters perhaps as skilled in physical as in spiritual coercion. The catastrophic end of the expedition demonstrated to the full the importance of speed and manœuvrability.

The galleon form persisted through Jacobean and Caroline times; ships became much larger, but without the clumsiness of older giants. The great ships in which Blake and De Ruyter fought were formidable craft. A ship of the line at the time of the Civil War would be about 130–140 ft. long by 35 ft. in the beam. As for sheathing, there was brief use of lead in the reign of Charles II, but the seventeenth century ships that Pepys knew so well had the bottoms coated with tallow or tar mixtures, containing hair, felt or ground glass, over which thin fir planks were fixed. Astern were mounted quarter-galleries, and during the Caroline years these were covered in and furnished with windows. Thus improved, they appeared as highly ornate oriels and demi-pavilions on each quarter, though in utilitarian fact they served their old purpose and contained the officers' water-closets. Latrines for the crew were in the beak, hence the persistent nautical term, "the heads", for such places. Save for a sober reaction during the Commmonwealth, decoration showed the full exuberance of Baroque architecture adapted to the style of a ship. The projecting stern gallery was a foreign feature, but recessed galleries were used on British ships into the late eighteenth century. Continuous decks replaced the up-and-down decking, high forecastle and poop of the traditional galleon, sheer was much less, and as the seventeenth century declined and the eighteenth advanced, naval craft began to assume what we think of as the Nelsonian form, which persisted until the coming of the iron-clad. Copper sheathing was tried in the seventeen-sixties, in Anson's time, but its teething troubles were resolved only when copper instead of iron bolts were used to secure the hull. Shipworm was most destructive of unsheathed vessels, especially in the tropics.

As to the size of eighteenth-century ships, the most famous of them all, H.M.S. *Victory*, built to the designs of Sir Thomas Slade during 1759–65, was 2,162 tons burthen, with length of keel 153·1 ft. and breadth 51·5 ft. At the time of Trafalgar she had been somewhat modified in detail, with the stern galleries gone, and she then mounted two sixty-eight-pounder carronades on the forecastle, ten twelve-pounders on the quarter deck and thirty on the upper deck, twenty-eight twenty-four-pounders on the middle deck and thirty thirty-two-pounders on the gun deck —one hundred guns complete.

For a long time the seagoing merchant ships continued to be well equipped with guns; in the parlance of later years the old East Indiaman might have been termed an armed merchant cruiser, which in our experience has meant anything from the enemy's description of a tramp he has just torpedoed to a ship of some puissance against all but heavily armed warships. The East Indiaman of the late eighteenth century was the largest of contemporary merchantmen, excelling anything in the

American trade. She carried guns on the upper deck and more guns on the 'tween-deck, with two stern chasers aft. She might be painted with dummy ports below, to deceive the less educated sort of marauders into thinking they had a man-of-war to deal with. Her sheer was very slight, and so was her tumblehome; the bow was round, the stern contained cabin windows in two tiers. Decoration was subdued, compared with the gorgeous fancies of former years, and this applied to naval craft also.

Passengers were not yet pampered, even in the austerest puritan sense of the word. Unless they were very special personages, they knew their place as a sort of human extra-freight. Their accommodation was improvised as required by the ship's carpenter. Slavers, sailing between West Africa and the Americas, carried men and women under conditions as horrible as in that Black Hole of Calcutta, with far longer duration, battened down in darkness, stench and disease. The strongest survived, and were sold at high prices.

Ordinary passengers were ordered about, and made to keep out of the way; their sufferings when seasick excited the derision of mariners; ("It's only a passenger!" said Robert Louis Stephenson's amiable Steward Blackwood). Regency and early Victorian artists portrayed them in comic drawings of astounding coarseness. But people were beginning to travel. In literature, Defoe's classic *Robinson Crusoe* (mariner) of the seventeenth century gave place, in the nineteenth, to Captain Maryatt's well-meaning but helpless Seagraves (passengers) in *Masterman Ready*, and to the quite preposterous *Swiss Family Robinson*. The literary and poetic lore of the sea has belonged chiefly to the English-speaking world. Joseph Conrad, who was a Pole, furnished the great exception, and he was a sailor who spoke, thought and wrote in English.

From volumes back to vessels; one other form of merchantmen of this period requires particular mention. Bluff, stout and tubby, the collier brig took coal from the Tyne to the South of England, to the Hanseatic ports, and even farther afield. She had, of course, great hold space relative to her size; her cabin accommodation was small and grim, her forecastle grimmer. She had other uses beside the transport of sea-coal. Captain James Cook's *Endeavour* was a collier.

Cook is our paragon among sea captains of all sorts during those centuries from the beginning of Tudor to the unexpected Victorian zenith of Hanover, a great sailor, a great explorer and an humanitarian whose end, however tragic, was fitting. The typical sea captain of his time and before was at best a martinet—as often he needed to be—and at worst a ferocious and sometimes murderous tyrant. Sir Walter Raleigh, for all his elegant gallantry at court, is reputed to have been the original of the cruel captain in the song of the *Golden Vanity*. Sir Richard Grenville, in spite of Sir Henry Newbolt's verses about sick men being brought aboard, *very carefully and slow*, was perhaps the most savage of the Elizabethan commanders, who, in his jollier moments, is said to have entertained the wardroom by eating fire and chewing up glass tumblers. Admiral Benbow was a fearsome man, a proletarian who had risen by a mixture of courage and ruthlessness. When he ordered that *a cradle with all haste on the quarterdeck be placed* so that he could continue to fight the French personally, with his hat on, while the remains of his leg were removed, he was practising what he preached. Bligh was not extraordinary; he is remembered because he had a mutiny with various peculiar consequences. Nelson may have considered it impossible to command a fleet without the periodic business of flogging a seaman nearly to death, yet we see him very cheerfully on the binge with his brave tars (fig. 125) and some Turkish visitors besides, and everyone of his company, from Captain Hardy to the powder-monkeys, was grief-stricken at his death.

Conquering Steam

So we come to the latest book in the Saga of the Ship. It covers little more than a century and a half, and it contains so much that this must be but a sketch of a sketch. Wooden walls went out. Steam came in.

A ship independent of wind or oars was a dream of mariners through several centuries (*cf.* Oliver Onions's eerie story "Phantas", in which the derelict galleon *Mary of the Tower* encounters a destroyer, within hailing distance, and otherwise only four centuries between them). There are many claims and records in the genesis of marine engineering; there were the attempts of Velasco de Garay in sixteenth-century Portugal; the eighteenth century saw those of Papin and de Jouffroy in France, of Hulls in England, of Miller and Symington in Scotland, of Fitch and Oliver Evans (who distantly anticipated the amphibian of World War II —the DUKW) in America.

The atmospheric steam engines of Newcomen and Watt served eighteenth-century industry, but not until Richard Trevithick made successful high-pressure engines did locomotion become possible, whether by water or by land. The steamer began, not as a challenger to the great ship, but simply as a new kind of craft for use in narrow waters. With the engine was necessary some sort of propulsive wheel, whether it were Hulls's rotating paddle or an adaptation of the Archimedean screw, for which various claims occur in the lore of ship propulsion. The first practical steam craft, William Symington's *Charlotte Dundas* of 1801 (fig. 146), which proved her slow but undoubted ability as a tug on the Forth and Clyde Canal, had a single-cylinder horizontal engine driving a paddle-wheel placed centrally in the stern. The central paddle-wheel persisted in the *London Engineer* of 1818 (fig. 151).

Robert Fulton's experiments bore fruit in the United States, and while it is easy to laugh at the Boeotian lines of his *Clermont* (fig. 148), and shudder at stories of red-hot boilers and other oddities about her engine, she became, in 1807, the first commercial steamer in the world, plying on the Hudson between New York and Albany. The next noteworthy steam vessel was Henry Bell's *Comet* (fig. 149), the world's first seagoing steamer. She plied regularly between the Clyde and Oban and Fort William before she was wrecked in Loch Craignish in 1820.

While non-condensing engines persisted, steam was fallible at sea, and was regarded largely as auxiliary to sail. The first steamer to sail an ocean from coast to coast was the American ship *Savannah*, a barque with an auxiliary engine and collapsible paddle wheels, which crossed from Savannah to Liverpool, May 24th– June 17th, 1819. The engine was working for only 85 hours. The first two all-steam voyages across the Atlantic were made simultaneously in the early summer of 1838. Of the vessels that made them, *Great Western* was a splendid ship of her day, one of the creations of I. K. Brunel, who built her namesake railway in England, indeed she was part of a spectacular "Paddington, Bristol and New York" scheme. She was built of oak, copper-bottomed, and stout as a line-of-battle ship. Her length was 212 ft. between perpendiculars, her extreme breadth, excluding paddleboxes, was 35 ft. Quite otherwise was her rival, *Sirius* (fig. 152), a little channel steamer which sailed from Cork to New York by chance, grossly overloaded. Fortunately there was no storm; otherwise, but for inestimable Providence, only *Great Western* would have arrived. *Sirius* reached the Hudson on April 22nd, having taken 18 days 10 hours from Ireland. *Great Western* arrived next day, having taken 15 days 15 hours from Bristol. She made sixty-four Atlantic crossings between 1838 and 1846, and was then sold into the West Indian trade. A second Brunelian prodigy was *Great*

Britain of 1843, of 3,270 tons gross, the first Atlantic liner to be built of iron, and the first with screw propulsion. She was a splendid steamer, and although not always a lucky one, she lasted for many years, becoming a sailing ship in 1882. She became a coal hulk at Port Stanley, Falkland Islands, in 1886. Thence rescued, long after, she is now back at Bristol as a cherished monument. Iron ships began with John Laird in 1829.

The world's navies at first looked askance at steam. The Royal Navy for some years would regard it only as an auxiliary. The 'sixties saw the proving of the steam ironclad, and the days of the tall ship of the line were ended at last. In the American Civil War, first use was made of the ironclad turret ship, invented by John Ericsson. The stormy Six Weeks War of 1866 saw the first great engagement between two large steam navies, those of Austria and Italy, off the Isle of Lissa (figs. 204–208).

In merchant shipping, there was a steady increase in the size and speed of ships. The prodigy was Brunel's third and last ship, the *Great Eastern*, of 1859 (figs. 179–182), for forty years holding the record of being or having been the largest ship in the world, of 18,915 tons gross register, 32,000 tons displacement, overall length 692 ft., breadth (excluding paddleboxes) 82·7 ft. She had both screw and paddles, the former of 24 ft. diameter and 37 ft. pitch, and the latter (originally) 56 ft. in diameter. Even so she was underpowered, she was a bad sea-boat, and was a wretched failure in passenger service. But she made an admirable cable ship with her vast capacity, and laid, among many others, the first two successful Atlantic cables (1865–66). A skeleton—some say two skeletons—were discovered in her false-bottom when she was broken up during 1888–90, which, in the opinion of old-time sailors, fully explained all her misfortunes.

The great storm of 1861, in which the *Great Eastern* had her paddles broken, helped to demonstrate the unsuitability of the paddle wheel for ocean service. Its efficiency was variable according to the amount of water the vessel was drawing, and it was extremely vulnerable. In war service the screw was indispensable for any large ship: a lucky shot amidships could disable a paddle-steamer in an instant. On the Atlantic crossing paddles went out, largely through the influence of Inman of the Inman and International Line. "Inman's Screws" were famous ships of their day. In the present century the seagoing paddle steamer has survived only in certain coastal waters, such as the Clyde, the Bristol Channel, the Thames estuary and the English South Coast, and it is near vanishing point now.

A beautiful feature of the Victorian era was the phase of the clipper ship, the fastest, and in her way the most splendid thing ever under sail. Considered broadly, the clipper was a highly refined East Indiaman. She was built for speed, with a very high ratio of length to breadth, and when speed was desired, an enormous amount of canvas could be set. She was the last tribute to the providence of the Trade Winds—out by the Cape, back by the Horn. To describe her loveliness under a full spread of canvas is impossible; at close quarters she was superb; miles distant she dominated the seascape.

The clipper of the late nineteenth century sprang from America about the time of the 'forty-nine Gold Rush, and during the 'fifties was copied and modified by British yards for the China tea and Australian wool trades. Coaling difficulties on such long runs gave advantage to the great sailing ship. The China tea clipper was of composite construction, i.e. planked and copper-sheathed on iron frames. The wool clipper was of iron. They were generally three-masters, ship-rigged, i.e. with square rig on all masts, but in later years the four-masted barque—three masts square-rigged and the after mizzen rigged fore-and-aft—was not uncommon. There were many variations, and the large ship rigged fore-and-aft throughout—the great schooner—was favoured by American owners.

In the 'seventies began the decline of the sailing clipper, for the opening of the Suez Canal gave the advantage to steam on the far eastern runs, but for years the tall ship clung to the Australian trade—wool and later grain. Claud Muncaster's classic *Rolling Round the Horn* was to the address of the Finnish ship *Olivebank*, which only ended her days, by the agency of a mine, in the war of 1939–45. A fast clipper could make as much as 18 knots in a good wind, and of the famous *Thermopylae*, on the Australia run it was said that she made 7 knots in a wind that was too light to disturb a candle on deck.

But steam was the conqueror; ships became bigger, and faster, and the early twentieth century saw the realization of the giant liner which Brunel and Scott Russell had attempted in the *Great Eastern*. Iron gave place to steel. Engines changed; the nineteenth century had seen the progressive use of compound and multiple expansion, but Charles Algernon Parsons's little turbine steamer *Turbinia*, which staggered people at the Diamond Jubilee Review of 1897 by zipping down Spithead at 34 knots, demonstrated the engines of ships to come.

Warships became heavier, faster and more powerful. The range of big guns grew longer. The war of 1914–18 showed another pointer to change. The giant warship, formidable though she were, was so expensive and so difficult to replace rapidly that the world's Admiralties grew cautious about risking her loss. Russia felt the first shock in 1904, when the incalculable Japanese Navy inflicted staggering damage. In the 1914–18 war, the fast, solitary sea-raider came back into her own, as did the submarine—child of nineteenth-century phantasy—which blockaded by sinking everything that crossed her path. Full-dress naval battles were memorable for their rarity. At Coronel, Admiral von Spee almost annihilated Cradock's cruiser squadron, and soon after was himself wiped out south of the Falkland Islands by Sturdee. Off Jutland, the German High Seas Fleet inflicted severe losses among our ships, but retired, itself somewhat mangled, not to reappear in that war. Late in the war, the first aircraft-carriers made their appearance, and their kind probably will be the last of the giant warships. The spear-head was now under water and in the air. The Battle of the Atlantic, in the long, bitter years from 1941 onwards, and the maintenance of the Russian convoys, were won by destroyers, frigates and corvettes, and above all by the fortitude of sailors, but were nearly won by submarines. Germany's giant battleships spent most of their war lying up in remote fjords; in one of which the *Tirpitz* perished miserably. When the *Bismarck* came out to do battle in the North Atlantic, it was to die fighting, as most people knew in advance. The star of the great battleship was setting at last.

The big cargo ship will always be with us, and the giant, fast liner remains as yet, in spite of passenger and freight aircraft that make the Atlantic crossing measurable in hours. One recalls the shuttlecock of the Blue Riband—*Mauretania —Bremen—Rex—Normandie—Queen Mary—United States*, and many others. Radar and comparable aids have revolutionized navigation, just as earlier in the century radio telegraphy revolutionized communication at sea. There have been more changes in the engine-room; the oil-engined ship challenges, though it has not succeeded in superseding, the large oil-fired turbine-driven steamer.

It is impossible to give an adequate review of modern shipbuilding and marine engineering progress within these few introductory paragraphs, so let us close by remarking a curiosity. Contemporary ship propulsion began, as we have seen, with the *Charlotte Dundas*, over a century and a half ago. She was a steamer. The U.S.S.

Nautilus, popularly described as an "atomic" submarine, was commissioned in September 1954. No furnaces here; instead, a nuclear reactor. But the *Nautilus* was also a steamer, for her screws were operated by steam turbines.

Thy Safety Being the Motive

Beacons and lighthouses, of a sort, have been known since the days of republican Rome. The Pharos of Alexandria (*c.* 300 B.C.) is the common classic in our history, but the Romans built similar light-towers in other places. They guarded the commerce of the first of the great modern empires, roughly two thousand years ago. "Modern" is there used in its widest sense; in some ways the Rome of the Caesars must have been rather like Chicago in the nineteen-twenties, without motor-cars, but with baths, beautie shoppes and gangs galore. The first lighthouse of our time was the Tour de Cordouan at the mouth of the Garonne, which was completed early in the seventeenth century. And that gives us a link with ancient Alexandria, for the French word for a lighthouse is *phare*.

In England, we owe to Henry VIII the original incorporation of Trinity House, which is to this day responsible for English lights, buoys and pilotage, having a senior status in relation to the Commissioners of Northern Lighthouses (Scotland and Man) and the Commissioners of Irish Lights. The original Dungeness Lighthouse, the first English light for which a toll was levied, was built under letters patent granted by James I and VI. In later years, isolated lights guarding rocks and reefs were added to the shore lights. The succession of Eddystone lighthouses is shown in figs. 392–395. Earliest illuminants were braziers, and use was made of huge iron chandeliers before the introduction of oil.

Late in the eighteenth century came two revolutionary improvements. One was the use of parabolic reflectors; the other, their mounting, with the lamps, in a revolving frame. Dioptric light, from a central burner and focused through lenses, was first produced by Augustin Fresnel in 1819. A logical development of catoptric (reflecting) and dioptric (refracting) systems was not unreasonably called cata-dioptric light, and involved, on the revolving lantern, reflection by outer prismatic rings and refraction by inner rings forming a central lens. The original light might be from improved Argand burners or, later, incandescent burners. The prodigy was the intensification of the light. One of the Trevose lighthouse keepers astonished your then younger author, about 1920, by remarking that he could not see to read in the lantern room, yet each night, the flash from Trevose Head was a wonder in the eyes of a boy.

Improvement of lighting by compressed gas made possible the use of light buoys to mark out channels and give warning of shoals. The bell-buoy and the whistling buoy lifted up their eerie voices in fog and darkness. During the nineteenth century the light-ship came widely into use. Probably no craft offers a more isolated and less comfortable life to her company than the moored light vessel. In some waters, notably in the Persian Gulf, unmanned lightships, or light-floats, serve their robot mission. For all the violent motion which is their norm, lightships rarely encounter accident, though the tragic end of a South Goodwin lightship is fresh in the memory, among all the things that have happened on the dreadful sands.

Quite another sort of safeguard was inspired by the gross overloading of ships by cynical owners in early Victorian years. Samuel Plimsoll was not a sailor. Sometime brewery manager, and later coal merchant, he was brought by the latter business in contact with shipping, and it inflamed his reforming zeal. He entered Parliament. He was righteous, quarrelsome and bitterly vindictive, the very model for an angry back-bencher of the Left. Those mixed qualities made him the Seamen's Friend and the mortal enemy of those who grew rich on "coffin ships". More than once he brought uproar to the Commons before his Merchant Shipping Act of 1876 imposed condign penalties on the owners of unseaworthy craft, and made obligatory the painting of load lines, of the familiar "Plimsoll mark", on all vessels.

Out of peril, by fear, are born ingenuity, defence and protection. The cruelty and the fantastic expenditure of war stimulate them. The ping of the asdic betrays the hidden killer; on the radar screen the invisible is seen. Yet the highest ingenuity of scientist and engineer is not enough without humanity, and to humanity above all we owe that wonderful social phenomenon, the Life-boat Service.

In days past, the attitude of coast dwellers to any sort of wreck was simply predatory. Survivors might be succoured—Spanish castaways in 1588 are said to have brought the art of making gay garments to Fair Isle in the Shetlands, though outside the bull ring one thinks of Spain as a country of black—black hats, black cloaks, black mantillas. But be it confessed that on the fierce coasts of Britain, the wreck was the thing, and that luring a ship on to rocks by false lights, if wind and a lee shore were not enough, was part of the business.

Yet the life-boat came. Selfless preparation for sacrifice made it possible. Royal patronage helped it. Sir William Hillary, founder of the Life-boat Service, in 1824, described it as a cause addressing itself with equal force to the best feelings of every class in the state. The organized altruism of Victorian England and the puritanism of Victorian Scotland both helped. Things like Grace Darling's exploit off the Longstones supercharged public imagination, and so, to give it its due, did some melodramatic verse of Wordsworth and of lesser poets who might not know a cleat from a bollard. We, the British, may search our souls today, wondering whether we are secretly proud, or deeply ashamed, of the fact that the Royal National Life-Boat Institution is an organization entirely dependent on voluntary support. For so it is.

In all the records of heroism at sea—of Grenville engaging an entire fleet with one old ship, of Victorian soldiers dying on parade as a trooper takes her final plunge, of men fighting fishing craft against blindly ferocious Nature, of men fighting battered corvettes against a superior and invisible enemy, of men fighting fear on a blazing tanker—in all the infinitely bitter range of things the sea hurls at adventuring mankind—the life-boatman comes second to none.

1. From the tomb of Mekhet Rā: Models of the King's travelling boat and its kitchen tender, with leadsmen forward and steersmen aft.

2–3. Noah's Ark: *Right* is Raphael's panel in the Vatican, with Shem, Ham and Japheth under paternal direction. *Below* is a cinema version by Warner Brothers, of the Ark's 'tween-decks, with the Old Man comforting seasick long-horns, and one of the pythons half-way down the main companionway.

4. Part of a Phoenician bireme, *c.* 750 B.C., from a contemporary relief.

5. Egyptian ship on Queen Hatshepsut's expedition to Punt. The anti-hogging truss is clearly shown; the giant squid among the fish suggests waters south of Sokotra.

6. *Below:* Athenian trireme at the time of the Battle of Salamis (480 B.C.).

7. *Above:* Reconstruction of Greek warships at the time of the Peloponnesian War, fifth century, B.C. Noteworthy are the anchor and cleats.

8. Greek warships engaging, fifth century, B.C.

9. Forepart of an Alexandrine galley at the time of the Battle of Actium (31 B.C.), from a contemporary relief. The crocodile was not a real one; it was Queen Cleopatra's ensign.

10–11. Left is a nineteenth-century reconstruction of Roman galleys, and below is one of the landing of Julius Caesar near St. Margaret's Bay, 54 B.C.; British armoured division of the period in retreat (left background). The shallow draught of Roman warships made instant beach fighting possible.

12–13. Roman trireme, first century A.D., after a wall painting at Pompeii and, below, another cinema reconstruction of Roman luxury ship and tender of the time of Nero (A.D. 54–68). Unlike the Pompeian picture, it shows anchors mounted both sides with the chains passing through hawsepipes. ("*Idonea tempestate nata et sublatis ancoris——*")

14. "The grandeur that was Rome." Remains of one of Caligula's pleasure galleys.

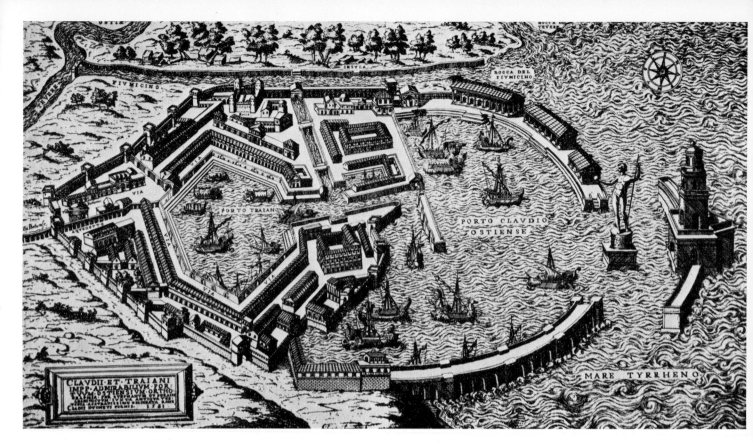

15. Port layout was advanced under the Roman Empire. Traditionally the first lighthouse was at Alexandria, but there was a handsome one at Ostia, shown in this sixteenth-century reconstruction of a first-century installation. Noteworthy are the long moles of the Outer Harbour, built by the Emperor Claudius (A.D. 41–52) and the Inner Basin of Trajan (A.D. 98–117).

17. Roman merchantman, second century A.D., from a model in the Science Museum, South Kensington.

16. Roman merchantman, from a second-century bas-relief. The supplicated deities are shown suitably large, and so is the All-seeing Eye.

18. Pre-historic is the coracle, here seen in a modern photograph taken below the bridges at Carmarthen. In quaint contrast are the mediaeval bridge and the Victorian railway signals.

19. The kayak of the Eskimos is another craft produced by primitive people, but far from primitive in construction and manœuvrability. The man here shown is not in an ideal position relative to the narwhal, which has a nasty look in its eye. (From Jules Michelet's *La Mer*.)

20. Little sister of the Viking ship is the boat still to be seen on the fjords and mountain tarns of Norway. (Picture "Jealousy" by Hans Dahl.)

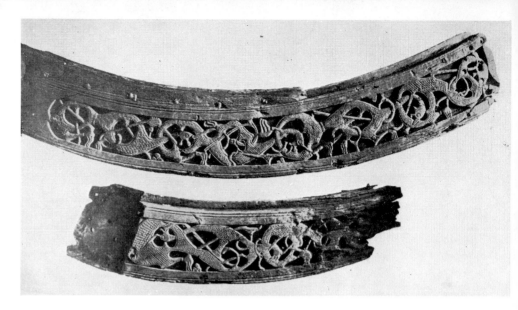

21–22. Figurehead and carved stem contemporary with the Oseberg Ship (ninth-century Norse).

23. Survivor of the Viking Era: The Oseberg Ship at Oslo, after having been ceremonially buried in the ninth century, preserved in the peat, and recovered in 1904.

24. Stern and steering oar of the Gokstad Ship, *c.* A.D. 900.

25. The ocean-going *Hafskib* of the Vikings. In the foreground are two ships very close, not a two-master. Painting by Marcus Randall.

26. Norse ship, time of Alfred the Great. This drawing presents rather clumsily the stem and figurehead, and the sheer is exaggerated.

27–28. The ship in contemporary art: Above is an eleventh-century painting of a Danish squadron being bothered by mermaids. Below is the invading fleet of William the Conqueror bound for Pevensey in 1066 (from the Bayeux Tapestry).

29. Norman ships, in a nineteenth-century aquatint.

30–31. Art and caricature: On the left, a highly conventionalized and compressed ship on the thirteenth-century seal of Dover; right, the same in a Victorian cartoon by John Leech for *The Comic History of England* ("Unpleasant position of King Harold").

32. Seaborne invasion, time of Henry III. Substantial wooden castles and small fighting tops for bowmen are in general use. On the right, horses are being unloaded by a remarkable anticipation of the twentieth-century landing craft. The lack of visible opposition and the presence of a lady suggest that a good beach-head has already been secured.

33. Fourteenth-to-fifteenth-century English warships, showing, right to left, progressive development of forecastle and poop. The three-master has arrived.

34. Ships of the late fifteenth century. The four-master has appeared, with two lateen-rigged mizzens; the forecastles are high and ungainly; abaft the mainmast is the cabin, with poop above.

35. Fifteenth-century English three-master with forecastle, summercastle and three fighting tops. The purely conventional decoration of shields along the bulwark derives from the actual shields which were ranged on a Norse ship. This vessel is clincher-built, but she has a proper rudder.

6–38. Saracen influence brought in the lateen sail, which belongs to Mediterranean craft today as of yore. Above is a Maltese galley of the sixteenth century. The middle view is from a nineteenth-century lithograph and shows Spanish martanes off Europa Point, Gibraltar. Below is the Nile in 1856, a scene that is almost ageless.

39. *Left:* Model, in the Science Museum, of the Portuguese three-master *Santa Maria*, ship of Christopher Columbus (Fig. 40, *above*). This, in Nargeo's engraving from Antonio del Rincon's picture, is believed to be the only *authentic* portrait of Columbus. There are many others.

41–42. *Below left:* Fernao de Magalhães (Ferdinand Magellan) led the first expedition to circumnavigate the world, himself losing his life in the course of it, 1521. *Below:* A Portuguese ship of the period. The numerous flying-fish seem to be suffering a combined offensive of dolphins, men and frigate-birds.

44. A less serious version of the Hanseatic ship. Holbein's original, rather improper drawing has been censored in this print, but it still has its curiosities; one of the mariners has chosen a peculiar place for a quiet drink.

43. Visby, Isle of Gothland, in the sixteenth century, from a Swedish painting by Admiral J. Hägg. A Hanseatic merchant-man is being towed into harbour by two boats.

45. Reconstruction (c. 1750) of the *Henri Grace à Dieu* (the second "Great Harry"); time of Henry VIII. The representation suggests rather the *Ark Royal* (see 52).

46. Queen Mary and Queen Jane, 1553.
Attack on the Tower of London by the Duke
of Suffolk. Drawing by George Cruickshank
from Harrison Ainsworth's "Tower of London".

47. Spanish galleon, late sixteenth century.
Huge and elaborate, she was a formidable
craft, but vulnerable to close attack. The
Spanish Armada was an invading fleet with a
large army aboard, rather than a battle fleet.
The picture is mid-Victorian.

48. Coming of the Invincible Armada, *alias* the Enterprise of England, 1588; on the left is a galleass, on the right a Portuguese caravel, with large galleons in background (nineteenth-century engraving).

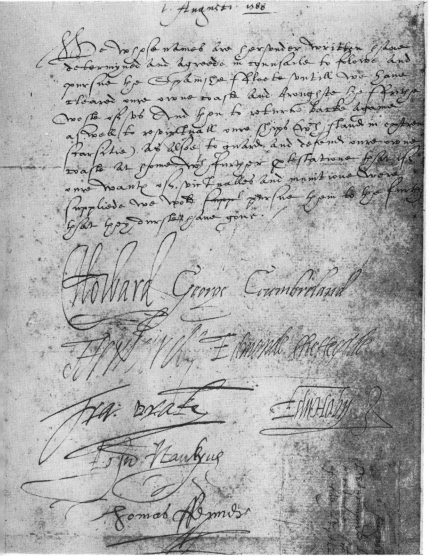

49. Defeat of the Spanish Invincible Armada; Signatures of the English admirals. Noteworthy is the fierce, impatient calligraphy of both Drake and Hawkins.

50–51. *Left:* The Lord High Admiral, Charles Howard, Earl of Effingham. *Right:* Admiral Sir John Hawkins.

52. One version of the *Ark Royal*, Howard's flagship, a four-masted galleon with gun-ports on three decks.

53. Pursuit of the Spanish Armada, from a contemporary painting in the Queen's House, National Maritime Museum, Greenwich. A large Spanish ship is foundering in the left background. In the foreground an English ship (*left*) is engaging and about to board a galleass.

54–55. *Left:* Admiral Sir Martin Frobisher, 1535–94. *Right:* Sir Walter Raleigh, born, 1552; put to death by James I, 1618.

"O eloquent, just and mightie death! Whom none could advise, thou hast perswaded; what none hath dared, thou hast done; and whom all the world flattered, thou onlie hast cast out of the world and despised. Thou hast drawne together all the farre stretched greatnesse, all the pride, crueltie and ambition of man, and covered it all over with these two narrow words, *hic jacet*!"

(Raleigh's *Historie of the World*)

56–57. *Above* is an engraving by Visscher, generally considered as representing the *Ark Royal*. This was purchased in 1587 from Sir Walter Raleigh, who had built her on his own account as the *Ark Raleigh*. On the left, the Invincible Armada is being harried up the Channel (de Loutherbourg, in the National Maritime Museum, Greenwich).

58–59. The Honourable Member for Plymouth, Admiral Sir Francis Drake. On the right he receives the sword of de Valdez, aboard the captured *Capitana* off Torbay.

60. Drake, with the *Revenge*, boarding the *Capitana*. (From a tapestry destroyed in the burning of the Houses of Parliament, 1834.)

61. First blood, 1588. The *Revenge* tows the *Capitana* into Torbay. (Engraving from a painting by O. W. Brierly.)

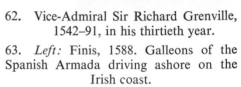

62. Vice-Admiral Sir Richard Grenville, 1542–91, in his thirtieth year.

63. *Left:* Finis, 1588. Galleons of the Spanish Armada driving ashore on the Irish coast.

64. The *Revenge* goes down off the Azores, after engaging a Spanish fleet of 53 ships for fifteen hours; 1591.

65. Sir Francis Drake, his burial off Porto Bello, January 28, 1596.

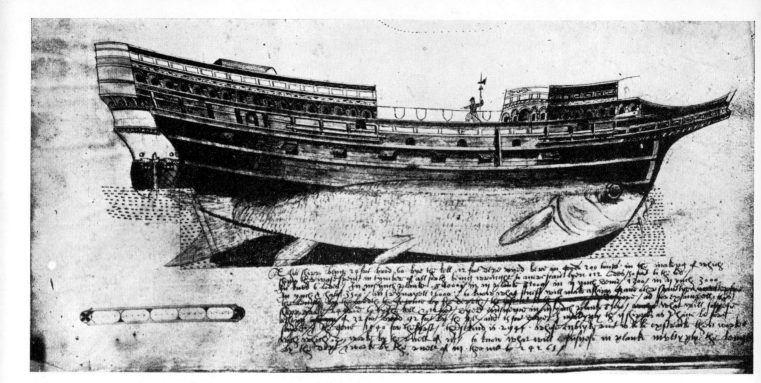

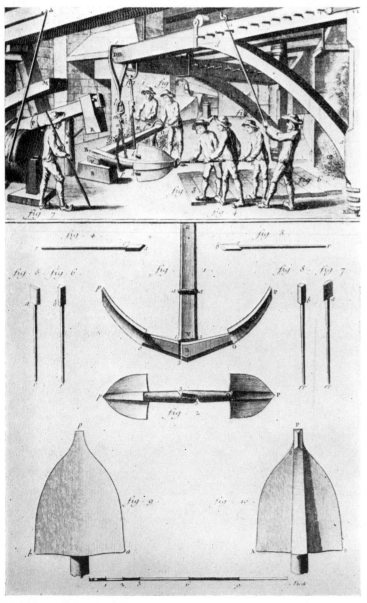

66–67. The making of a ship. *Above:* Theory of streamlines, c. 1600; the ideal form had the head of a codfish and the tail of a mackerel. On the left, forging an anchor in a dockyard smith's shop of the eighteenth century; details of the flukes below. Noteworthy, in the smith's shop drawing, is the cam-operated hammer, probably worked by water power.

68. The *Sovereign of the Seas*, a Caroline ship of the line, with the heavy decoration of the mid-seventeenth century. Engraving by J. Payne after Peter Pett the Younger.

69. At the Admiralty in the reign of Charles II. Close to the stern of the model is Samuel Pepys, Secretary to the Admiralty; with him are John Evelyn and Lord Sandwich (taking snuff). Painting by Seymour Lucas: "A Whip for the Duteh".

70. Rembrandt's "The Shipbuilder and his wife". (By gracious permission of H.M. The Queen.)

71–72. With the rise of the Dutch Republic came the rise of the Dutch painters, whose superb pictures of shipping remain second to none. Into them went all the art and the pride of a people that had found itself after throwing off long years of Inquisition frightfulness. Above is a painting of galleons in a storm, now in Buckingham Palace; below is the Four Days' Battle of June 1–4, 1666. Both are by Van der Velde.

73. The Dutch attack on Chatham, 1667. Admiral de Ruyter has just captured the *Royal Charles*, and has hoisted the Dutch tricolor. Other English ships are burning. It was a great triumph and a great disgrace. Picture by Jan Peters.

74. Admiral Robert Blake, 1599–1657. (Miniature by Samuel Cooper.)

75. Admiral Adrian de Ruyter, 1607–76.

76. Battle Royal: Van Diest's picture of the Four Days' Battle between Monk and de Ruyter in the Channel, 1666. The Royal Navy lost nine ships and the Dutch fifteen.

77. H.M.S. *Resolution*, flagship of Admiral Sir Thomas Allin, Commander-in-Chief, the Mediterranean, 1669. Picture by Van der Velde the Younger. Early appearance of the first Union Flag on the mainmast. The painting admirably shows the elaborate decoration of the stern and quarters. Painting in the Queen's House, National Maritime Museum, Greenwich.

78. Dutch ships off Amsterdam, by Van der Velde.

79. The Glory of France. Jean Bart escorts a Polish wheat convoy safely from the Baltic to Dunkirk, repelling a massive Dutch attack off Texel. (Engraving after the painting by Isabey at Versailles.)

80. Battle of La Hogue, 1692; burning of *Le Soleil Royal*. Louis XIV of France had assembled a Franco-Irish invasion force under ex-King James II and VII, and Admiral Tourville. Attacked by an allied British and Dutch force, it made a great fight, which nevertheless ended in a French disaster.

81. Vice-Admiral Sir George Rooke, 1650–1709. His firing of French ships at La Hogue gained him his knighthood and £1,000 a year. He is said to have been embittered by the greater adulation of Marlborough. Portrait by Dahl in the National Maritime Museum.

82. At the close of the Stewart Era; H.M.S. *Royal Sovereign*, launched in the first year of Queen Anne; Rooke's flagship at Cadiz, 1702.

83. Ship section, eighteenth century. Tom's engraving of a two-decker. Head-room between decks was just sufficient for a medium man. From the false bottom rose the stink of the bilges. The square-rigged fore- and mainmast, with the lateen-rigged mizzen, went back to the late fifteenth century.

84. *Below:* Bow, heads and forecastle of a 60-gun ship, *c.* 1760.

85. Galleried stern of H.M.S. *Ipswich*, 70-gun ship of 1730, from a model in the National Maritime Museum.

86. Admiral Lord Anson, 1697–1762; Ridley's engraving of Reynolds's portrait. Bold, acquisitive and resolute, he was yet generous. He wrote of his adversary, La Jonquière: "I ought to be satisfied, but wish he had had a little more strength, though this is the best stroke that has been made upon the French since La Hogue."

87. Admiral Lord Hawke, 1705–81. He received his first command (H.M.S. *Wolf*) at 29. Following Belle Isle (1747) he was made K.B. and Vice-Admiral of the Blue. Quiberon Bay, 1759: Vice-Admiral of Britain, 1765.

88. Anson's voyage round the world, 1740–44. H.M.S. *Centurion*, last survivor of the squadron, captures the Spanish treasure-ship *Acapulco*, with cargo worth half a million. The drawing is of later date.

89. On May 3, 1747, soon after the last Jacobite rising, the Royal Navy acquired by capture *Le Sérieux*, which became H.M.S. *Intrepid*.

90. Quiberon Bay, November 20, 1759; Hawke's attempt, with the *Royal George*, to rake the *Soleil Royal*, is being frustrated by the *Intrépide* coming up to receive his fire. Picture by D. Serres in the National Maritime Museum.

91. Cap Rouge, Quebec, whence General Wolfe dropped downstream on the ebb tide to capture the city, September 13, 1759.

92. Defeat of the allied French and Spanish fleets in Gibraltar Bay, 1782; attack by fire-ships.

93. Raising of the siege of Gibraltar by Lord Howe, October 11, 1782. Painting in the National Maritime Museum.

94. An East Indiaman of the late eighteenth century. She was the contemporary equivalent of an armed merchant cruiser and is seen here in the Downs, bound for India under the first (Anglo-Scottish) version of the "Red Duster".

95. Clarkson Stanfield's "The Morning after the Wreck". A Dutch East Indiaman dismasted and stranded.

96. Lord Howe in action with the French fleet off Ushant, 1794 (the "Glorious First of June"). De Loutherbourg, in the National Maritime Museum.

97. Independent piracy, chiefly by English, Dutch and French captains, swelled during the early eighteenth century, and for years, pirates dominated the Caribbean. The unacknowledged Confederacy of Buccaneers, which had become immensely rich, was supposed to have been broken after the Peace of Rijswijk, 1697, but the pirates still pursued fortune.

98. The Pirate at the Bar. Captain Kidd before the House of Commons 1701. He had been granted letters of marque to suppress piracy and harass the French, but entered the business himself. People are still looking for his fabulous hidden hoard.

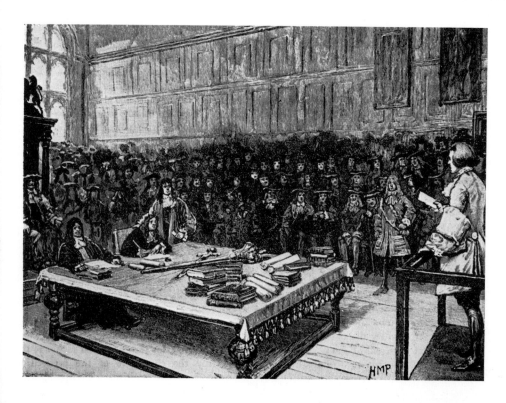

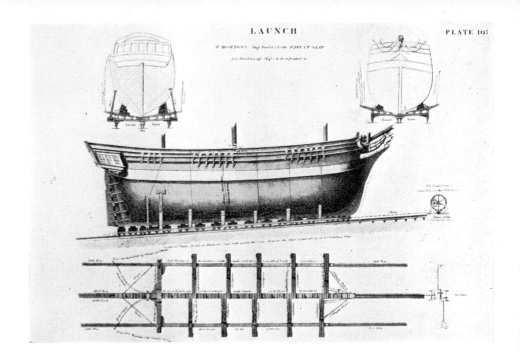

99–101. Shipyards: The uppermost view shows Morton's patent slip, designed for hauling up a large ship for repairs and refitting; in the middle is H.M.S. *Nelson* on the ways before launching; below, H.M S. *Prince of Wales* takes the water at Portsmouth. The lowermost view is more amusing than accurate; the sheer of the ship is exaggerated and the figures are out of proportion. There has been no change in the ritual of launching.

102–103. Captain James Cook ; Dance's portrait, engraved by Holl; on the right are Cook's ships *Resolution* and *Discovery* off Vancouver Island. Cook is conventionally remembered as an explorer, but he was foremost among the great humanitarians.

104–105. In five hundred years there was little change in the Northern Chinese junk, which preserves a mediaeval form even now. For several centuries, too, there was little change in the Chinese captain.

106. It is doubtful who first thought of the floating dock, but its purpose, in part, was originally served by an old hulk. This example was off Rotherhithe in the eighteenth century.

107. London's East End, mid-eighteenth century. Old East India Wharf, London Bridge, in a picture ascribed to Samuel Scott. The Indiamen are berthed beyond the drays; the warehouses stand in dingy Georgian dignity; the largest visible crane is worked by convicts through a treadmill.

108. The Pool of London in the early part of the eighteenth century. Many of the vessels are collier brigs from the Tyne.

109. Singleton's "An Ocean Swell". The girl on the left may be carrying the cauliflower as an added inducement.

110. "Good News of the Boy". (Eighteenth-century Dutch.)

111. American War of 1812: Action between H.M.S. *Shannon* and U.S. *Chesapeake*.

12. "The Chace of a Cutter." Pouncey's engraving after Kitchingman, 1783.

113. A "seventy four", early nineteenth century.

114. Maltese cutter, late eighteenth century.

115. Napoleonic Wars. Captured British midshipmen on the French coast. Painting by W. J. Yeames.

Cet animal est très méchant
Quand on l'attaque, il se défend!

116. "Jack Tar", 1807.

117. A post captain, time of Nelson.

118. Lord Nelson, his commands: *Left to right:* H.M.S. *Agamemnon* (Toulon, Corsica), *Captain* (St. Vincent), *Vanguard* (The Nile), *Elephant* (Copenhagen), *Victory* (Trafalgar).

119. Battle of St. Vincent, February 14, 1797. Commodore Nelson (H.M.S. *Captain*) leads a boarding party on to the Spanish ship of the line *San Nicolas*. He lost his sword arm off Teneriffe in the following year.

120. Admiral Viscount Nelson of the Nile, Duke of Brontë, 1758–1805. His uncle, Maurice Suckling, Comptroller of the Navy, taught him the art of the *scientific sailor*.

121. Cuthbert, Admiral Lord Collingwood, 1750–1810. He took command at Trafalgar on the death of Nelson. A model sailor in little as well as great things, he is said to have carried acorns in his pockets, and scattered them as he walked the countryside, that there should be always plenty of British oak.

122. Admiral John Jervis, Earl of St. Vincent, 1735–1823. His victory over the Spanish fleet off Cape St. Vincent in 1797 was that of a man facing nearly twice his own strength.

123. The Battle of the Nile, August 1, 1798. Explosion of *l'Orient*. (George Arnald in the National Maritime Museum.)

24. The Nile: a solemn moment: From I.M.S. *Vanguard* Nelson watches the destruction of the French flagship *l'Orient*.

125. A less solemn moment: "Nelson recreating with his brave tars after the Battle of the Nile". An apocryphal drawing.

126–127. Bombardment of
Copenhagen, April 1, 1801. It was
here that Nelson put the telescope
to his blind eye, but the signal he
chose to disregard was an invita-
tion, not a command. In the upper
view, the Danish ship of the line
Dannebrog blows up. In the lower
Nelson sends a dispatch from
H.M.S. *Elephant*. Upper picture
after J. P. Serres; lower by Thomas
Davidson.

128–129. Nelson leaves England. He boards his admiral's barge for the *Victory* on May 18, 1803 (painting by Andrew Gow in the Royal Exchange). *Below:* Trafalgar, October 21, 1805.

130. Turner's "The Death of Nelson".

131. After Trafalgar. H.M.S. *Victory* towed into Gibraltar Harbour (Clarkson Stanfield).

132. H.M.S. *Victory* in Portsmouth Harbour; late Victorian times.

133. Restoration of H.M.S. *Victory* in the nineteen-twenties. When her critical state became public knowledge, all sorts of strange expedients were proposed, from her demolition on moral pacifist grounds to her dismemberment and reconstruction in Trafalgar Square. She was docked for good, and restored to her 1805 state, as shown in Wyllie's painting in the National Maritime Museum. Beyond is H.M.S. *Queen Elizabeth*.

134. Trafalgar jug in the National Maritime Museum. Such a battle had all sorts of commemorations. China figures of Nelson, more or less libellous, adorned cottage mantelpieces, and fearsome portraits were hoisted as inn signs. This jug, however, is of considerable merit, and carries a plan of the battle.

135–136. There remained the Barbary Corsairs, their heirs and assigns. *Left:* Parley between Lord Exmouth and Omar Pasha, August 29, 1816, two days after the bombardment of Algiers. *Below:* Napoleon was on St. Helena; France had been occupied by British and Germans; yet the paradox was that the Barbary menace only ended with the French moving into Algeria.

137. End of a wooden wall; H.M.S. *Foudroyant*, broken-backed on Blackpool sands, a spectacle for proletarian curiosity.

138. Gun deck on the *Constitution*. Trajectory was regulated by the timber chocks below the gun barrels.

139. With dignity and with a last gesture of defiance, H.M.S. *Implacable* went down in the Channel in 1949, with 152 years behind her. A seventy-four, as the French ship *Duguat Trouin*, she fought the *Victory* at Trafalgar and was captured. Rotten at last with age, she was sunk off Selsey Bill, flying the White Ensign and the Tricolor. Horizontally split by the demolition charge, she left her poop and upper deck awash.

140-143. Ancient was the figurehead, but it reached its perfection under the Regency. Above on the left, the *Black Prince* fights a marine Cressy; right, *Ajax*, now in the National Maritime Museum, stares mournfully after his old ship; below, the great Duke from H.M.S. *Marlborough* submits to the cosmetic treatment of a far-on generation, and on the right is a maiden lady in retirement at Southwold—a Victorian *Bacchante*, bearing grapes but wearing trouserines.

144–145. *Above:* The dawn of steam: Jonathan Hulls's attempt (1736–37) to produce a tug powered by a Newcomen atmospheric steam engine. On the *left* is Bourne's lithograph of Patrick Miller's double-hulled steamboat on Dalswinton Loch, 1788. She was engined by William Symington.

146–147. *Right and below:* Symington's steam tug *Charlotte Dundas*, Forth and Clyde Canal, 1802. She towed two barges of 70 tons burthen 19½ miles at 3·6 m.p.h. Steering was by capstan, cabled to two rudders. The view, *right*, shows a model in the Science Museum, South Kensington, with the single paddlebox removed to show the wheel.

148. Robert Fulton's *Clermont* looked as if she had been built by a man who knew little about mechanics and less about a ship, but on the Hudson in 1807 she was the world's first steamer in regular commercial service.

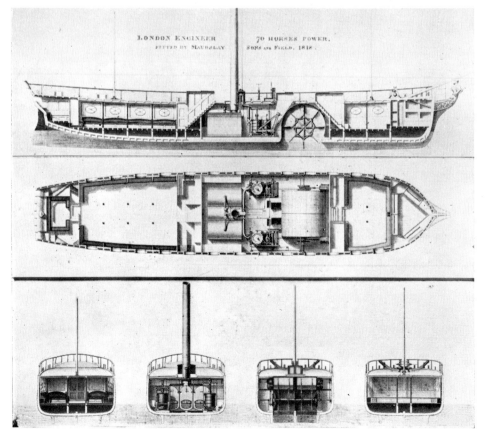

149. *Centre left:* Henry Bell's *Comet*, built on the Clyde in 1811, worked the first passenger service by steam in Europe, between Glasgow, Greenock and Helensburgh (January, 1812). Later she worked the world's first seagoing steam service, to Oban and Fort William, and was wrecked on this run in 1820. She was engined by John Robertson (150, *above*), here seen with the engine.

LONDON ENGINEER   70 HORSES POWER.
FITTED BY MAUDSLAY   SONS AND FIELD. 1818.

151. Sections and plan of the saloon steamer *London Engineer* of 1818. She had two single-cylinder Maudslay engines driving what might have been called "sociable" paddle wheels through bell cranks and connecting rods.

152. *Sirius*, the little Irish Channel packet built in 1837, which was the first ship to cross the Atlantic entirely under steam (Cork to New York, April, 1838). She took 18 days 10 hours, burnt up all her coal, and when she made landfall had also consumed the cabin furniture, doors and one mast.

153–154. *Centre and right:* A few hours after *Sirius* docked, Brunel's handsome *Great Western* followed her, arousing fresh excitement at the sight of so large a steamer from the Old World. She had sailed from Bristol, and made the run, more comfortably than *Sirius*, in 15 days 5 hours, or at an average of 8·8 knots. She consumed 655 tons of coal, but docked with 200 tons still in the bunkers.

155. So steam came to the Atlantic run. Here is the *British Queen* of the British and American Steam Navigation Company.

156–157. *Centre:* Samuel Cunard's first steamer *Britannia*, 1,154 g.t., made her maiden voyage in July, 1840. Icebound at Boston, Mass., in February, 1844, she was released by a seven-mile channel cut through the goodwill of the Boston merchants, a generous gesture by the Tea-party city. *Above:* Sir Samuel Cunard, 1787–1865.

158. The Indian Mail service was inaugurated from Southampton by the Peninsular and Oriental company's steamship *Hindostan*, of 2,017 tons. She sailed on September 24, 1842.

159. Irish Mail steamer *Cambria*; Chester and Holyhead Railway Company, 1848. From an early date, railway companies owned fleets in the narrow seas, and maintained very high standards.

160. A handsome wooden steamer of her day was the P. and O. company's *Bentinck*, built in 1843 for the Suez-Calcutta run. She had a maximum speed of 12 knots, but all her coal had to be brought from England round the Cape.

161. Proudest of early Victorian steamships was the splendid iron screw-steamer *Great. Britain*, launched at Bristol in 1843. Another of Brunel's ventures, she was divided by six water-tight bulkheads. This picture shows her original six-masted schooner rig.

162. At first, steam made little difference to the aspect of the Royal Navy, especially as funnels could be taken down when out of use. At a glance, this view up Portsmouth Harbour shows little change since Nelson's days.

163. Grand Harbour, Malta, in mid-Victorian years. On the left are the Sardinian ship of the line *Vittorio Emanuele* and H.M.S.s *Neptune* and *Cressy*. On the right is H.M.S. *Marlborough*.

164. S c r e w versu paddle. April 3, 1845 saw a spectacular tug-of war between H.M. Sloop *Rattler* and *Alecto*. Apart from engines, the vessel were similar but the *Rattler* tugged the protesting *Alecto* nearly three miles, stern-first in a calm sea.

165. Steam ship of the line *Agamemnon*, launched at Woolwich in 1852. She was typical of the phase under which the Royal Navy still regarded steam as an auxiliary power.

166. H.M.S. *Agamemnon*'s most famous assignment was the laying of the first Atlantic telegraph cable, from Ireland to Newfoundland, together with H.M.S. *Leopard* and the U.S. Ships *Niagara* and *Susquehanna*, 1857–58. This woodcut shows *Agamemnon* on her beam-ends in the great storm of June 20–21, 1858.

167. The ships that passed: Turner's *Fighting Temeraire*. Like many lesser painters, Turner has exaggerated the proportions of hull to masts. The picture is further interesting as a very early illustration of an Admiralty tug.

168. Golden age of the clipper: *Ariel* and *Taeping* off the Lizard, 1860; they left China on the same day; they reached London on the same day.

169. Clippers racing up Channel. Painting by A. Chidley. This and the succeeding views convey something of the extraordinary beauty of the great sailing ship in its last years.

170. Four-masted barque *Archibald Russell*. Painting by A. Briscoe.

171. From the pilot boat.

172. Three-masted ship *Doughless*. Rig, forward to aft: Outer jib, inner jib and fore topmast staysail; foresail, lower fore-topsail, upper fore-topsail, fore-top-gallant and fore-royal; main-topmast stay-sail, main-topgallant staysail, and main-royal staysail; mainsail (brailed up), lower main-topsail, upper-main topsail, main-top gallant and main skysail; mizzen-topgallant staysail, cross-jack (furled), lower mizzen topsail, upper mizzen-topsail, mizzen-top-gallant and mizzen-royal, spanker.

173. Trinity Wharf on London River, July 15, 1866.

174. Trinity House buoy wharf, Black-wall, 1868.

175. Tea clippers in East India Dock London, late nineteenth century; not whiff of steam in sight.

176. Four-masted ship *Olive Branch*, by A. Briscoe.

177. Victorian passengers on a sailing ship, middle 'eighties. In calm weather it was the laziest life in the world. Little intrigues flourished; a single lady could enjoy herself.

178. London dockside pub. Drawing by Gustave Doré. Gin and rum were cheap; there were thieves, harpies and murderers galore. Classic descriptions occur in Morrison's *The Hole in the Wall* and Dickens's *Our Mutual Friend*.

179. Prodigy of Victorian shipbuilding was the *Great Eastern*, 22,500 tons, for nearly half a century the largest ship in the world, and a hoodoo ship most of the time. She achieved success as a cable ship, and laid the first successful Atlantic cable in 1866, also recovering the 1865 cable which had broken.

180–181. *Above left:* John Scott Russell, Hervey Wakefield and Isambard Kingdom Brunel at the launching of the *Great Eastern*, November 3, 1857. Launching was not complete until January 3, 1858; the ship's misfortunes had begun on the ways at Blackwall. *Centre right:* She is at quayside in New York, probably in 1867. The painting of the paddlebox is bad enough for modern times.

182. Many believed that so big a ship as the *Great Eastern* could not possibly roll. This was her grand saloon, September 12, 1861. A goose is mixed up with the passengers and furniture, and a cow is coming through the starboard skylight.

183. The hydrographic survey ship, H.M.S. *Challenger*. A corvette of 2,306 tons, she covered 68,900 nautical miles on a voyage lasting from December 7, 1872 to May 24, 1876.

184. Loss of the troopship *Birkenhead* off Simon's Bay, February 26, 1852. Of a company numbering 638 persons, 184 were saved in the ship's boats. The ship sank so rapidly that there was little time for getting on parade.

185. Steam versus piracy: H.M.S. *Virago* taking the pirate schooner *Eliza Cornish* in the Straits of Magellan.

186. H.M.S. *Warrior*, ironclad battleship, launched on December 29, 1860; at that time the second-largest ship in the world.

187. Coming of the Ironclad—end of the wooden-walls. Two battleships off Sheerness in the eighteen-sixties.

188. H.M.S. *Nymphe*, a Victorian steam sloop.

189. Iron, steam and sail. In the Victorian Era, the old-time figureheads representing personages and animals, vanished from the Royal Navy, in favour of the Royal Arms, following the example of H.M.S. *Victory*.

190. *Above:* The Mississippi steamboat of the mid-nineteenth century was a craft of unique regional design. Not only was there nothing like her at sea; there was nothing like her on the Hudson, the Rhine, the Danube or the Volga.

191. *Left:* Up the bayou: A small Mississippi-type stern-wheeler used as a pleasure craft by Thomas Alva Edison.

192. On the Mississippi: "Set her back!" Pilot, Horace Bixby; cub-pilot, S. L. Clemens ("Mark Twain").

193. Transhipment at New Orleans in the eighteen-sixties; seagoing vessels in far background, river steamers at the levee. River navigation on the treacherous Mississippi was apart, and is honourably included in this otherwise salty chronicle. Half a continent depended on it; the steamboatmen referred to others as "landsmen".

194. Arrival of a load of cotton at New Orleans;
time of the Confederacy.

195. *Above:* Most famous of American raiders in the Civil War was the Confederate ship *Alabama* (Captain Semmes). Built at Birkenhead, she did enormous damage to United States mercantile shipping between July, 1862, and June 19, 1864. On the latter date she was engaged and sunk off Cherbourg by the U.S.S. *Kearsage* (Captain Winslow).

196. *Left:* United States steam frigate *Kearsage*, lying in Cherbourg roads after the *Alabama* action.

197. The *Trent* Affair, November 8, 1861: Captain Wilkes in the U.S. frigate *San Jacinto* stops the British Royal Mail steamer *Trent*, and takes prisoner Confederate Commissioners on their way to Europe. It nearly brought Great Britain into the war on the Confederate side. Ruffled British plumes were smoothed next year when Captain Wilson of the blockade-runner *Emily St. Pierre* overthrew a Federal prize crew and brought his ship to Liverpool.

Above: Both fleets in the American Civil War were at first old-fashioned
and traditional. The Confederates produced, in the *Merrimac*, a sort of armour-
plated steam Noah's Ark. The Federal
navy built *Monitor*, John Ericsson's
revolutionary turret-ship. They met noisily
and indecisively in Hampton Roads,
March 9, 1862.

Right: A monitor to the rescue:
U.S.S. *Monadnock* takes a disabled gun-
boat in tow, during a storm off Cape
Hatteras.

200. Ericsson monitor-type ships in
action with the Confederate ironclad
frigate *New Ironsides*.

201. United States monitor-type sh[...]
Dictator, 1863. This view well demo[...]
strates the raft-like aspect of these extr[...]
ordinary craft.

202–203. *Centre left:* In the State[...]
war raged up the Mississippi from Ne[...]
Orleans, and Vicksburg was besieged b[...]
land and river. The broad, shallow-draugh[...]
Mississippi steamboat took on a new[...]
redoubtable form. *Above* is Admir[...]
David Farragut, U.S. Navy (1801–70[...]
victor of Mobile Bay.

204. In the war of 1866, Italy an[...]
the Austrian Empire had each a fleet i[...]
transition from wooden-wall to ironclad[...]
For the first time in history, two larg[...]
battle-fleets met under steam. *Left* is th[...]
Austrian steam-ram *Kaiser Max*.

205. Lissa, July 20, 1866. On the left, the Italian ironclad steam-ram *Palestro* is on fire; it reached the magazine and she blew up. In the middle distance the *Ferdinand Max* has just rammed the *Re d'Italia*, which sank in three minutes, a victim of the bungling of Admiral Persano who signalled "Port your helm!" when he meant "Port your wheel!"

206–207. *Above:* Admiral Baron von Tegetthoff, the victor of Lissa. *Centre, right:* The Austrian wooden steam frigate *Radetsky*.

208. Battered by Tegetthoff, the Italian fleet limped home with three ships lost. Humiliation was not yet complete; Persano's darling, the new battleship *Affondatore*, foundered in Ancona Harbour during a storm soon after the action off Lissa.

209. In the years following the American and Austrian wars, the armoured turret ship advanced a long way from Ericsson's original design, but the Royal Navy was reluctant to abandon all sail. Here is H.M.S. *Inflexible*, proudly brig-rigged.

210. Warships for shallow waters could border on the freakish. Even in the middle years of last century, the New Zealand stern-wheel gunboat *Rangiriri* was the sort of craft at which one looked twice.

211. Royal Salute. H.M.S.s *Galatea* and *Raccoon* at Simon's Bay on a visit of the Duke of Edinburgh, August, 1867.

212. The changing shape of the battleship. Malta in 1878: H.M.S. *Thunderer* in left foreground, a new turret ship.

213. In the French battleship *Massena* we see transition in several directions. She was a steam-ram, with blistered hull and old-fashioned gunports.

STERN VIEW, SHEWING RUDDER & SCREWS

214. Freak battleships were not wanting in the early days of heavy armour. Admiral Popoff advanced the circular vessel ("steam saucer"?), several examples of which were built by the Russian Government, beginning with the *Popoffka Novgorod*, launched at Nicolaieff in 1875.

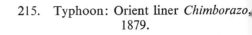

215. Typhoon: Orient liner *Chimborazo*, 1879.

216. Peril: "Short-handed"; engraving after Lionel Symthe, 1874.

217. Horror: Burning of the American steamer *Golden Gate*, July 22, 1862. There were 100 survivors from a company of 33?

218–219. Worst disaster in the history of London River was the collision of the S.S. *Bywell Castle* with the P.S. *Princess Alice* in Gallions Reach, September 3, 1878. The big collier was scarcely damaged, but the paddle steamer, much overloaded, was cut in half and sank immediately. Above is the *Illustrated London News* two-page plate from the week following; on the right is the after part of the *Princess Alice* beached near Woolwich. Over 650 lives were lost.

220. Unusual among collisions was that of the Glasgow sailing ship *Lochearn* with the French mail steamer *Ville de Havre*, November 22, 1873. The great French ship sank in twelve minutes, with the loss of 226 lives. *Lochearn*, sinking nearly a week later, had been abandoned, and her company rescued by the *British Queen*. British and French courts disagreed over responsibility.

221. East India Docks, London; eighteen-seventies.

222. Greatest of the Cunard paddle steamers was *Scotia*, 3,871 tons, with two-cylinder side-lever Napier engines. Launched in 1861, she held the Atlantic Blue Riband from 1862 to 1867.

23. Even through the
ter decades of last cen-
ry, many people dis-
usted a ship without sails.
his was the P. and O.
Britannia.

24. Suez Canal, built by Ferdinand
Lesseps, 1859–69 ; (Verdi's opera
ida was commissioned to celebrate it).
he canal reduced the distance between
ondon and Bombay to 6,442 miles, com-
red with more than 11,000 miles round
e Cape. This view probably dates from
e early 'nineties; coming through is
H.M.S. *Malabar*.

25. Ships in the Hooghly;
eighteen-seventies.

227. Much ado. Collision between the American coastal passenger packet *Bristol* and the British barque *B. Rogers*. At the time there seemed nothing particularly funny about the parade of contemporary underwear.

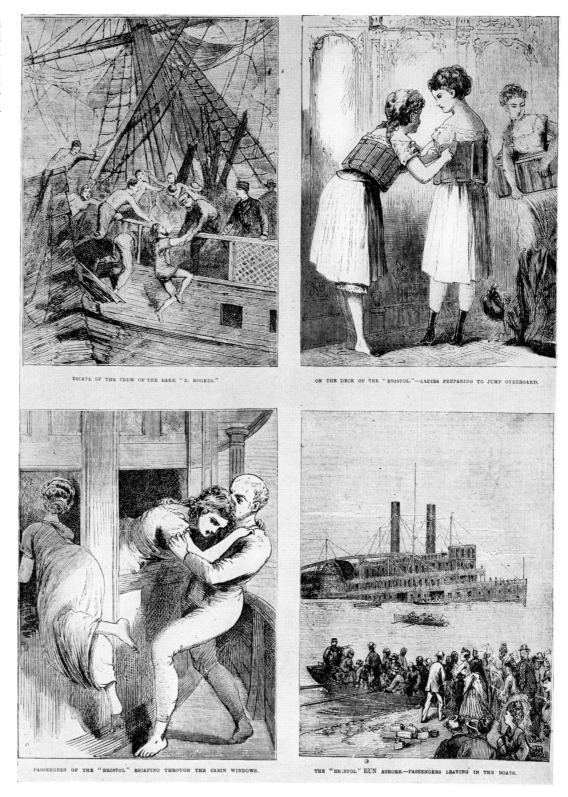

ESCAPE OF THE CREW OF THE BARK "B. ROGERS."

ON THE DECK OF THE "BRISTOL."—LADIES PREPARING TO JUMP OVERBOARD.

PASSENGERS OF THE "BRISTOL" ESCAPING THROUGH THE CABIN WINDOWS.

THE "BRISTOL" RUN ASHORE.—PASSENGERS LEAVING IN THE BOATS.

Opposite Page

226. Was there ever a queerer craft, or a worse sea-boat, than the obelisk ship *Cleopatra*? The obelisk, made by Thutmose III (c. 1600 B.C.) was offered to the British Government as a token of esteem by the then Viceroy, A.D. 1877 (Sir Ralph Abercrombie had already bought it in 1801). It had this extraordinary vessel built round it at Alexandria, and it took four months on its voyage to London. Six lives were lost, and lost also was the *Cleopatra* for some time off Northern Spain. The three-funnelled ocean tug *Anglia* (*centre*) brought her from El Ferrol to London's Victoria Embankment, where her cargo has since been known as Cleopatra's Needle.

228. London sailing barge, mid-nineteenth century; painting by R. H. Nobbs.

229. Old paddle tug in Whitby Harbour. Craft such as this served as the first steam trawlers in the North Sea.

230. Sailing bargemen on London River, 1877; a fine example of a Victorian posed photograph.

31. Seaside pleasure-boats: *Skylark* and sister at Brighton.

32. Smack off Whitby; painting by David Hamilton in the Author's collection.

33. Old hoys at Ramsgate, *c.* 1890. The Margate hoy provided passengers and freight transport between London and Thanet, very cheaply, until long after the coming of steam.

234. Below Ben Nevis,
1888. Entering the Cale
donian Canal is the S.S.
Cavalier (1883–1927);
the paddle steamer is the
first *Mountaineer*, built in
1852, wrecked in the
Sound of Mull in 1889.
On the quay is the pre
railway Fort William bus.

235. "Doun the Watter";
Broomielaw, Glasgow, in
1885. In the foreground
is the Lochgoil steamer
Chancellor (1880); next,
in order, are Buchanan's
Vivid and *Eagle*, both
dating from 1864.

236–237.   Macbrayne's West Highland steamers. Above is the handsome clipper-bowed *Grenadier* (1885–1927) rounding the top of Kerrera on the Oban-Staffa-Iona run (painting by the Author); *right*, a Victorian scene at Rothesay with the famous *Columba*, Queen of Clyde paddle steamers (1878–1935).

38.   Highland travellers and tourists, 1871.

239. Ingenious device for preventing seasickness, *c.* 1878. One wonders at the reactions of the man at the wheel, also to what extent the five girls turned round on their axis, and how they mounted their cradle.

240–241. Achievement of anti-rolling was particularly sought on the Dover–Calais short sea route. Sir Henry Bessemer, wizard of steel, was a helpless victim of seasickness, and devised this ship with a self-trimming saloon in 1875. Ingenious the *Bessemer* was, but a hopeless failure. Her saloon was salved and became a handsome hall in an establishment for young ladies in Kent. A German bomb finished it in the nineteen-forties.

242–243. Most successful of the "anti-rolling" ships was the *Calais-Douvres*. Though slow, she was steady and comfortable, and passengers liked her. She had two hulls, with the paddle wheels between.

244. Drawing by G. Durand. *Les Victimes de Neptune*. The scene is the South Eastern Railway quay at Folkestone after a rough passage in 1874. Mother (with Narwhal's horn) is self-controlled. Grandmamma still suffers.

245. R.M.S. *Servia*, built for the reconstituted Cunard Steamship Company in 1881, a steel steamer of 7,392 g.t., won the Blue Riband of the Atlantic with a time of 6 days 23 hours and 50 minutes.

246. Hamburg in the eighteen-eighties. German girls, like our own, saw nothing incongruous about boating in bustle.

247. Inman liner *City of New York* at Southampton. The Inman fleet was sold to American interests; it also established Southampton as a transatlantic passenger terminal.

48. "The Stokehold", from Lloyd's "P. & O. Pencillings".

49. Another "P. & O. Pencilling": Sahib and Memsahib; steamer in the Bay; fiddles on tables; as yet, the punkahs are still.

250. Emigrants messing; eighteen-seventies. The smell of the crowded steerage reminded Robert Louis Stevenson of "some horrible kind of cheese".

251. End of a Hamburg three-masted barque, the *Carl*, in Constantine Bay, North Cornwall.

252. Fire down below! Burning cotton in the after hold of the S.S. *City of Richmond*.

253. An early tanker: S.S. *Volute* of the Shell company, 1893.

254. The tanker *Nerite* discharging the first cargo of liquid fuel at Suez, October, 1899. Mineral oils were used chiefly for lighting, and comparatively little for motive power; motoring was in its infancy, and oil-burning locomotives were rare except in parts of Russia. Few foresaw the future.

255. Manchester a seaport: Manchester Ship Canal was opened on January 1, 1894. The yacht *Norseman* passes the Barton swing-aqueduct. Seventy-one ships followed her on that day.

256. The earliest torpedo-boats of the Royal Navy curiously combined features of both the steam launch and the armoured steam ram, a much larger vessel (see 204–205 ante.)

257. *Above:* Collision between H.M.S *Collingwood* and H.M. training ship *Curaçao*, 1897. Drawing by Bernard Gribble.

258. The royal yacht *Osborne*.

259. Diamond Jubilee Review. Spithead, 1897. Pre-dreadnought battleships with, on extreme left, an earlier turret ship, and on the right. H.M.Y. *Osborne*. Painting by Charles Dixon.

260. *Below:* H.M.Y. *Victoria* and *Albert*, 1899, perhaps the final noteworthy example of what had already become an archaic type of steamship.

261. The passing of Queen Victoria, 1901. Royal yachts *Alberta*, *Osborne* and *Victoria and Albert*, the second-mentioned bearing the royal coffin; the German Emperor's yacht *Hohenzollern*; H.M. Battleships *Majestic* and *Prince George*; H.M. Destroyers 8 and 4. Drawing by W. S. Tomkin.

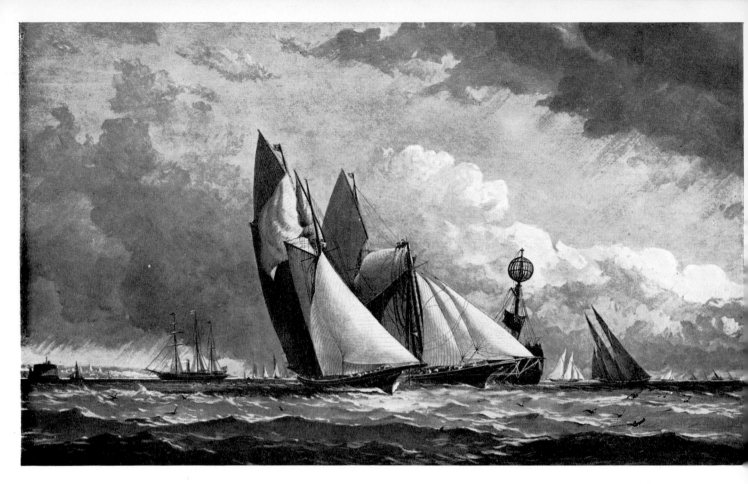

262–263.   Even in the days when sail was still all-important to commerce, the sporting side of sailing was realized and enjoyed. The upper view is from a mezzotint of a painting by Barlow Moore, of the mid-nineteenth century. Below is the cutter *Talisman* in her great race with the *Corsair* from Cowes round the Eddystone and back, 1842.

264. *Above:* Scarborough Regatta, 1895.

265. Cowes Regatta, 1894: *Valkyrie, Britannia, Inverna, Navahoe* and *Calluna.*

266. Steam and sail off the Kent Coast, 1894.

267–269. Whaling techniques changed with the century. Above is a whaler boiling down blubber (mid-nineteenth century); next comes a steam whaler, about eighty years after, with inflated "fish" in tow; below is an early whaling steamer, with harpoon gun. The modern whale-factory is a large ship with elaborate facilities for shipping the carcases, flensing and boiling (see 368).

270. The whaler had other uses. The late Herbert Ponting's photograph shows the *Terra Nova*, the ship of Scott's successful but tragic South Polar expedition (1910–12). Roald Amundsen was first in the dash for the Pole. Scott perished on the return, with his officers Oates, Bowers, Wilson and Petty-Officer Evans.

271. Sir Ernest Shackleton's *Endurance* drops down London River at the start of his South Polar Expedition. Shackleton returned. The ship it was that died, crushed in the ice-pack.

272. In 1904 the world watched modern naval warfare between Russia and Japan. Admiral Rozhestvensky's Second Pacific Squadron, on its way from the Baltic, distinguished itself by an incredible exhibition of naval hysteria, steaming into the middle of the Gamecock Fleet of Hull, which was fishing the Dogger Bank at midnight of October 22, 1904. The Russians blazed wildly at the trawlers, sinking the *Crane* and hitting five other vessels.

273. The Imperial Navy of Japan, 1904; Western science at the command of Eastern Empire. (Painting by Charles de Lacy.)

274. For a long time people had been wondering about the self-propulsive torpedo and its effect. During 1904 the Russians and Japanese both used it, and people found out. Here the Russian battleship *Rossia* has sent one into the Japanese trooper *Kinshiu*.

275–276. The vengeance of Japan: *Above:* The Russian ship *Variag* is sinking off Chemulpo (February 9, 1904), where she was caught with the *Konietz* at the outbreak of war. The French cruiser *Pascal* is standing by, having lowered boats and a steam pinnace. *Below:* Togo's Japanese fleet is in pursuit of Rozhestvensky's squadrons, which it destroyed.

277. *Above:* On February 21, 1907, the Prince and Princess of Wales opened Devonport Dockyard. The dressed cruiser is H.M.S. *Sirius* with a battleship beyond.

278–279. The early twentieth century saw the advance of the practical submarine. Above, *right*, is a British A class, and *right*, one of the E class which achieved fame in the years 1914–18.

280. The end of a changing era was shown in the three tall funnels of a County class cruiser. H.M.S. *Monmouth* was lost in 1915.

281. *Left:* H.M.S. *Dreadnought* off Portsmouth, 1906. Distantly on the left is H.M.S. *Victory*. Between is a naval paddle tug.

282. Dreadnought, H.M.S. *Thunderer*, 1912. She had ten 13·5-in. guns, sixteen 4-in., and three torpedo tubes. The arms-race with Germany was quickening. *Thunderer* was the last big ship from a Thames-side yard.

283. Far Eastern coastal liner: The *Kobe Maru* of the South Manchuria Railway, on the Dairen–Shanghai run *c.* 1910.

284. At the end of the nineteenth century, Germany made a strong bid for Atlantic dominance. The *Kaiser Wilhelm der Grosse* was a Blue Riband holder in her day. Built in 1897, she became an armed merchant cruiser, and was sunk by H.M.S. *Highflyer*.

285. Channel steamer, time of Edward VII. The second *Donegal* of the Midland Railway, on the Heysham–Belfast run. Built in 1904, she was sunk by enemy action in 1917.

286. Rivals to the Cunard Line, White Star commissioned the two giant liners *Olympic* and *Titanic*. The latter, here shown leaving Belfast for her speed trials, sank in collision with an iceberg, on her maiden voyage, 1912.

287. The Cunard liner *Mauretania*, 1907. She held the Blue Riband of the Atlantic until 1929.

288. In massive majesty, the Hamburg Amerika liner *Vaterland* leaves Hamburg on her maiden voyage, 1914.

LONGITUDINAL SECTION OF FERRY STEAMER

289–291. Train-ferries began on the Firth of Forth in 1850. The following decade produced this ambitious proposal for a ship with two train decks and hydraulic lifts, for the Channel. Passenger train ferries followed in the Danish narrows, and then between Sweden and Germany. The lower view shows the cradle between ship and railway at Trälleborg, Southern Sweden, and on the left is the train deck of the Swedish State train ferry *Drottning Viktoria*, built on Tyneside by Swan Hunter and Wigham Richardson in 1906.

292–293. Early history of the Panama Canal was both tragic and scandalous, and in 1889, after a decade of troubles, the original company was liquidated. The United States Government completed the task in 1914. The upper view shows the great Culebra Cut, and *right* are the Gatun Locks, with vessels being towed through by electric locomotives on a rack railway.

294. Less ticklish of the public fancy has been the Manchester Ship Canal (see 258), but here are the terminal docks of Manchester, a great city long miles from the sea, and with no river worth the name.

295. The Shell tanker *Vulcanus*, 1910, one of the very first seagoing motor ships.

296. Charles Algernon Parson's tiny steamer, the *Turbinia*, looked like a launch when she intruded on the 1897 Jubilee Review. But, in fact, she was a revolutionary.

297. Funnels, paddle-wheels and th[e] muddy Mersey; Liverpool–Birkenhea[d] ferries in the eighteen-nineties.

298. Cowes, 1914: Arnold Bennett wrote, on August 2: "It seemed to be monstrous that the glory of Cowes Regatta should be even impaired by fears of a war." The Regatta was abandoned by Royal Command on the third, and the country was at war on the fourth.

299. Fog, fish and flying gulls; a grey winter morning at Grimsby.

300. Dutch steam lifeboat (with net stern) standing by a large tramp steamer. (Painting by J. van Masterbrock.)

301. Eve of war: The German High seas Fleet in single line ahead, with a seaplane and a Schütte-Lanz airship escorting; 1914.

302. Vice-Admiral Count von Spee; victor of Coronel, killed off the Falkland Islands, December 8, 1914.

303. Admiral of the Fleet Sir Doveton Sturdee, victor of the Falkland Islands, Study by Sir Arthur Cope in the National Maritime Museum.

304. Battleship *Danton*; the French equivalent of a dreadnought.

305. H.M.S. *Hampshire*, torpedoed off the Shetlands, June 5, 1916, with the Secretary of State for War, Field-Marshal Earl Kitchener. Drawing by Charles Pears.

306–307. Dogger Bank, January 24, 1915. *Above*, H.M.S. *Arethusa* and the crippled *Blücher* (Bernard Gribble); *below*, *Blücher* capsizes (the all-time scoop photograph published by the *Daily Mail*).

308. Broadside; 1914–18. H.M.S. *Renown*.

309. The old battleship, H.M.S. *Camperdown*, as a submarine mother-ship

310. H.M.S. *King George V*, a super-dreadnought completed in 1912; 23,000 tons displacement, ten 13·5-in. guns.

311. Admiral of the Fleet Earl Beatty, D.S.O., O.M., 1871–1936.

312. Admiral of the Fleet Viscount Jellicoe of Scapa, O.M., 1859–1935.

313. Jutland Bank, May 31, 1916. *Left*, H.M.S. *Lion* (Beatty's flagship); *right*, H.M.S. *Queen Mary* blows up.

314–316. Having fought an indecisive prestige battle off Jutland, Germany bottled up her heavy ships. Her naval command realized, soonest of the combatants, the tremendous power of the submarine as a fighting and blockading weapon, while older schools regarded it as a rather indecent form of auxiliary. German submarine warfare was absolutely ruthless. *Above* are torpedo craft and submarines with their mother-ship; *next*, German submarines U 35 and U 42 at sea; *below*, a sister craft holds up a Spanish merchantman.

317. The Swedish barque *Samoa*, sunk by German submarine U 151, June 14, 1918.

318. German viewpoint: *Ein Volltreffer*.

319–320. R.M.S. *Lusitania*, torpedoed off Old Head of Kinsale, May 7, 1915. Intended by the Germans to impress Washington, the action angered the then neutral and loftily critical United States. (Drawing by Norman Wilkinson.) Ocean currents do queer things; *centre, right*, is a life-jacket from the *Lusitania*, hooked out of the Delaware at the foot of Race Street, Philadelphia, two years after the war.

321. On the spot: German battleship *Goeben*.

322. H.M.S.
Iron Duke in
floating dock,
August, 1933.
The ancient, and
in this case re-
suscitated, stern-
walk is clearly
shown.

323. Ostend,
May, 1918: The
last fight of
H.M.S. *Vindic-
tive*, sunk there
as a blockship
following the
blocking of Zee-
brugge. Drawing
in *The Sphere* by
Fortunino Ma-
tania.

324–326. H.M.S. *Furious*, improvised
aircraft-carrier, indicated in 1918 a strange
shape to come. The upper view was taken
from an airship; in the middle is an early
take-off by a Sopwith biplane with skid
undercarriage from a railed runway on the
flight deck; below is a close-up of *Furious*.
She carried a fighter squadron and a
Submarine Scout Zero airship, here seen
on the after flight deck.

327. Western approaches, 1917: A Coastal class (modified Astra Torres) airship keeps her majestic watch over an incoming convoy. An airship could spot, and even kill, a lurking submarine.

328. K class submarine: Steam on the surface, with battery-electric propulsion while submerged.

329. Camouflage of ships by dazzle-painting came into its own during the 1914–18 war, though it simply copied Nature, as in the coloration of certain animals. Here it has been applied to the old U.S. battleship *North Carolina*. The steel lattice mast was for long characteristic of the United States Navy.

330–331. Port of London: *Above* is S.S. *Fort Vercheres* discharging grain in Royal Victoria Dock; *below* is the Glen Line steamer *Glenorchy* in the entrance lock of King George V Dock.

332–333. *Above:* Greenwich Reach; the *Begonia* of North Shields with coal lighters alongside. *Below:* Like their namesake birds, the cranes of London bend acquisitively over a newly arrived ship, the *Port Wellington.*

334. White ships of the Baltic: Visby Inner Harbour, 1937. Left to right are the Svea Line steamers *Thjelvar*, *Visby*, *Drotten* and the stern of *Gotland*. (Compare with 43.)

335. The mirrored loch: Macbrayne's motor vessel *Lochiel* at West Loch Tarbert, 1950.

336. In coastal and estuarine waters, the paddle steamer long survived. She was a steady sea-boat and easily manoeuvrable. This was P. and A. Campbell's *Glen Gower* (1927) off Brighton in the nineteen-fifties. The naval type funnels were characteristic of the Campbell fleet.

337. The Fleetwood trawler *Cava* comes in after fourteen days in the North Atlantic. The trawl gallows are clearly shown.

338. Dunkirk, 1940. Against a sable backcloth of oil fires, the little ships embark an army. Visible in Charles Cundall's painting are a small motor cruiser, a steam collier, two Thames tugs, a paddle steamer and a destroyer.

339. The Hitler War: The armed liner *Jervis Bay* (right) goes into suicidal action against the battleship *Admiral Scheer*, while her convoy disperses. Painting by Charles Pears.

340. Destroyers dropping depth-charges. Painting by Norman Wilkinson, in the National Maritime Museum.

341. The German prison-ship *Altmark*, cornered and boarded by the British destroyer H.M.S. *Cossack*, in the cold night of a Norwegian fjord; February 16, 1940. (Norman Wilkinson, in the National Maritime Museum.)

342.   *Above:* Military landing-craft might be mistaken for the monstrous offspring of train-ferry and barge, but with them was accomplished the greatest sea invasion in modern history. This one, however, is at Hong-Kong, far from the Normandy beaches.

343.   Off St. Anthony's Light. Convoy entering Falmouth, 1942. Dazzle-painted frigate escorting, barrage balloons above. (Painting by John Platt in the National Maritime Museum.)

344. Battlecruiser H.M.S. *Hood*. In her day the largest warship in the world, she came at the end of the Kaiser's war. Her own end came in a thunderclap—a long shot from the *Bismarck*, herself fated never to return.

345–346. Sailors of the dark 'forties. *Left:* Submarine control room; H.M.S. *Stubborn*; painting by William Dring. *Right:* Stoker Martin of H.M.S. *Exeter*; portrait by E. Kennington. (Both in the National Maritime Museum.)

347. *Gotterdämmerung:* Sinking of the *Bismarck*; North Atlantic, May 27, 1941. Painting by C. E. Turner.

348. North Russian convoy entering Murmansk; painting by Norman Wilkinson in the National Maritime Museum.

349. The end of the *Scharnhorst*, September 26, 1943. Painting by Charles Pears in the National Maritime Museum.

350. St. Nazaire: H.M.S. *Campbelltown* steams in to her memorable suicide.

351. Under a dappled dawn, a Cape-town harbour tug persuades the Union Castle company's *Pretoria Castle*, bound for Southampton.

352. R.M.S. *Queen Mary* Cunard-White Star Line, 1934. First British ship over a thousand feet long, she gained the Blue Riband twice, making the run in 1938 in 3 days 20 hours 42 minutes.

353. Arrival of Her Majesty Queen Elizabeth II in Sydney Harbour, 1954; the liner *Gothic* as royal yacht. Painting by L. Wilcox in the National Maritime Museum.

354. All through the nineteen-forties, the Rotterdam-Lloyd liner *Willem Ruys* lay unfinished. The Germans are said to have marked her down for their own post-war services; The Western Allies did not bomb her; after the war her owners completed their ship.

355. New York, 1939: *Queen Mary*, *Normandie* and *Ile de France*.

356. The middle of the twentieth century saw the coming of a passenger steamer with her engines aft, like those of a tanker—and why not? The Shaw Savill liner *Southern Cross* runs her trials from Belfast in the Clyde below the Peaks of Arran.

357. Off the Lofotens: Norwegian motor trawlers.

358. Trawlers at Hull. There are no harder tasks, and no tougher life at sea, than on the trawlers and carriers, engaged in all weathers and at all seasons on the nation's fisheries.

359. Port of London: Unloading Baltic timber at the Surrey Commercial Docks.

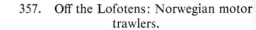

360. A small coasting tanker: *Shell Farmer* of the Shell-B.P. Group.

361–362. In the unquiet waters of the Minch and the Scottish West Coast, the ship has taken a form as local and as individual as that of the Baltic (see 334), but stouter and more dogged. These are two of Macbrayne's later motor vessels, the cargo ship *Loch Ard* and the mail and passenger ship *Claymore*, both serving the Outer Isles.

363–365. With the motor era, the tanker has become a great ship. *Above* is the British Tanker Company's *British Engineer*, of 32,000 tons d.w. *Right* is a weatherly view of the *Helicina*, looking aft; *below* the *Theodoxus* butts through the South Atlantic. Since our covered period, the tankers have become the largest ships in the world. *Oilbergs?*

366. Winter navigation in the northern seas is possible only through the constant patrol of ice-breakers. This is the Swedish ship *Ymer*. By hydraulic equipment she can rapidly alter her trim and break up the ice by pitching and rolling through it.

367. The Shell tanker *Volsella* takes the water at Cammell Laird's Birkenhead yard, 1950. As did the passenger ship, the tanker grows larger. This, and the ships on the facing page, were giants when they were commissioned.

368. Whales: The catcher brings the "fish" to the factory ship *Balaena*.

369–371. The magnificence of Edward's days: *Top, left,* is the great domed dining saloon of the *Lusitania,* which lies encrusted and algid off Kinsale. *Above and below left* are second-class cabins and first-class staterooms.

372–374. Saloon contrasts: Above is the first-class smoking-room on the *Donegal II* of 1904 (see 285), an Edwardian equation of ship, club and pub. In the middle is the uncomfortable elegance of the royal suite on the Swedish State train ferry *Drottning Viktoria*, 1906. On twentieth-century ships, furnishing and decoration has ranged from grand-hotel to plain ham, but beauty is on the *Willem Ruys* (see 354); here was her main companion-way, with its unique cuttlefish balusters and its famous mermaids. Last we heard of this elegant ship was that she was carrying Muslim pilgrims in Eastern waters.

375–376. New lines and different:
Left: Fred Olsen oil-driven liner *Braemar*
on the Newcastle–Oslo run; (*below*), in
London Docks, are the Orient liners *Orion*
and (*left*) *Orsova*. In the mid-twentieth century, masts dwindle to vanishing point.

377. Mid-century styling of the less
exaggerated sort, and aerodynamic funnel
design, characterize the P. and O. company's beautiful *Arcadia*, here seen steaming south through the Suez Canal.

378. At first sight, nothing previous in the lore of the ship has resembled the aircraft carrier. This is H.M.S. *Glory*.

379. Royal Review in Spithead, 1953; the battleship is in decline; beyond H.M.S. *Vanguard* lie the aircraft carriers. (Painting by Norman Wilkinson in the National Maritime Museum.)

0. H.M.S. *Loch Fada*: perhaps no single class of ship won any war, at least since Nelson's day, but the frigate certainly helped in the Second World War.

381. Grain: *John Anderson*, a floating elevator in the Port of London, with a maximum handling capacity of 300 tons p.h.

382–383. After early beginnings in the North, train ferries between England and the Continent began during the war years 1914–18; passenger train ferries followed between Dover and Dunkirk in October, 1936, but senior to these is the Harwich-Zeebrugge freight service, using old war-time craft in its earlier years. In 1947 was commissioned the *Suffolk Ferry*.

384. Advance of the cable ship: The *Recorder* of Cable and Wireless, Limited, built by Swan Hunter and Wigham Richardson, 1954.

385–386. *Above:* B. P. *Haulier* being launched sideways at Faversham, April 22, 1955. She was the first tanker to have Voith-Schneider propellers, and it was the first launch made with petroleum grease on the ways. *Right* is one of the propellers being shipped. This form was pioneered on the Lymington - Yarmouth motor ferry; it enables a ship to turn practically in her own length, and eliminates the traditional rudder.

387. The Glory of Sail. Bermuda sloop *Robbe* at Cowes, August, 1949.

388. Eighteen sail; Cowes.

389–391. In the yacht is art and mystery; in it we see the apotheosis of the sailing ship which economic history has used and passed over. *Left*, in the garden of the Royal Corinthian Yacht Club, Cowes, are Commodore F. G. Mitchell and Uffa Fox, designer and great artist. *Below, left*, is the Swedish-built *Llanoria*, winner of the 1949 Olympic Games Trophy; and *below, right*, Commodore Mitchell's *Noa* breaks out her spinnaker. These shots are all from the nineteen-fifties.

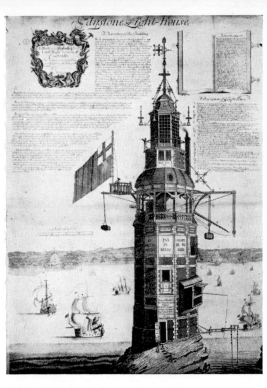

392. *Left:* Safety at sea: Winstanley's Eddystone Lighthouse, built in the late sixteen-nineties. It was destroyed, and Winstanley lost with it, in the great gale of November 27, 1703.

393. *Right:* In the dawn of marine humanity: Dutch sailor with rockets in the eighteenth century.

394. Eddystone: Smeaton's lighthouse of 1770. Engraving by Lipton, after Turner.

395. Eddystone: Sir James Douglass' lighthouse, built during 1879–82, with Smeaton's lighthouse, which it replaced. Smeaton's tower was re-erected as a memorial to him on Plymouth Hoe, 1882–84, and stands there still, looking across to its successor.

96–397. There is no more arduous, uncomfortable and evoted service than that of the light-ship men, moored in all eather at all seasons off the shoals and reefs of the narrow seas. Unmanned light-vessels are used in some foreign waters, notably in the Persian Gulf. On the right, such a craft is being loaded for the long journey to its Eastern station.

398. "Launching the Lifeboat", by T. Brooks; a picture full of the action and the personal drama of Victorian graphic art, which rarely forgot the wife, the sister and the mother. The boat is of an early self-righting type, but is far from invulnerable. The coxswain is pointing one way and the women looking another.

399. Lifeboat Coxswain Henry George Blogg, G.C., B.E.M. He served over 53 years, 38 years as coxswain; he went out 387 times and saved 873 lives.

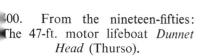

00. From the nineteen-fifties: The 47-ft. motor lifeboat *Dunnet Head* (Thurso).

401. Naval sea-rescue craft; nineteen-fifties.

402. Art and commerce; *Creole*, the Greek-owned staysail-schooner lent to Great Britain for the Torbay–Lisbon race of 1956; on the left, the *United States*, Blue Riband holder.

403. In far grey waters the met. ships keep their austere vigil, watching and warning us of what the winds will bring. This is the *Weather Recorder*, 300 miles south of Iceland, seen through the bomb doors of an R.A.F. Shackleton from Prestwick. The "bombs" were two canisters, containing Christmas mail and a Christmas tree.

404. The U.S.S. *Nautilus* was, and looked like, a very large submarine. It was less apparent that she was, like the old British K class, a submersible steamship, or that her turbines were supplied by a thermo-nuclear (or "atomic") steam generator.

405. Truly the last of the giant battleships, here is the U.S.S. *Missouri* (the "Mighty Mo"). Three naval tugs are nosing her up to No. 7 Pier at Norfolk, Virginia. Her ancestry is long. H.M.S. *Hood*, U.S.S. *Monitor*, H.M.S. *Warrior*, and more remotely the *Sovereign of the Seas* and the *Regent of the Tower* all stand in her lineage.

406. Not much of our planet remains unknown but still it has its mysteries. The autumn of 1956 saw the start of two expeditions in one ship; the Commonwealth Trans-Antarctic party and the Royal Society group visiting the South Polar regions for the International Geophysical Year. With these the Danish vessel *Magga Dan* leaves Tower Bridge Pier for the far end of the world.

Index

Figures in italic refer to page numbers in the Introduction; those in roman refer to the numbered illustrations

Acknowledgements

The author's sincere thanks are due to many people in connexion with the preparation of his second Picture History. He would record in particular the names of Commander A. C. Hardy, who read the original text, and offered the most helpful criticisms and suggestions, and of Mr. George P. Naish, of the National Maritime Museum, who most patiently went over the proofs, line by line, picture by picture, caption by caption. One could not have wished or hoped for better pilotage.

Further, he would like to recall the names of his childhood friend, the late Spencer Arnold, whose collection was acquired by the Picture Post Library, and of his brother, the late Christopher Ellis, who left a collection of photographs of British and French warships, made during the 1914–18 war.

This list gives the origins of the illustrations following:—
Author's Collection, 31, 213, 232, 234, 236, 251, 278–280, 282, 290–1, 304, 309–10, 334, 336, 369–71, 373
British Transport Commission, 158–9, 285, 372, 382–3
Cable and Wireless, Limited, 384
Cunard Steam-Ship Company, 156-7, 222, 245, 287, 352, 355
Fred Olsen Line, 375
H.M. The Queen's Collection, 70, 71
Imperial War Museum, 324–8, 342, 344, 378, 380
David Macbrayne Limited, 237, 335, 361–2
Manchester Guardian, 401
Mappin Art Gallery, Sheffield, 95

National Maritime Museum, 57, 75–6, 84, 90, 96, 120, 123, 133–4, 141, 228, 259, 261, 303, 339–41, 343, 345–50, 353, 379
Picture Post Library, 1, 2, 3, 5, 7–15, 18–29, 31–8, 40–2, 45, 47–56, 58–65, 67–9, 72–4, 77–83, 86–9, 91–4, 99–103, 105–13, 115–19, 121–2, 124–32, 135–40, 142–5, 147–55, 161–212, 214–21, 223–7, 229–31, 233, 235, 238–44, 246–9, 252, 255–8, 260, 262–77, 281, 284, 286, 288–9, 292–3, 296–302, 305–8, 311–23, 329, 337–8, 357–8, 387–95, 397, 398
P.A.–Reuter, 406
Paul Popper, 403
Peninsular and Oriental Steam Navigation Company, 377
Port of London Authority, 330–3, 359, 375, 381
Rotterdam-Lloyd, 354, 374
Royal National Life-Boat Institution, 339, 400
Science Museum, South Kensington, 16, 17, 30, 39, 44, 65, 85, 104, 114, 146
Shaw Savill Line, 356
Shell-Mex and B.P. Limited, 253–4, 295, 360, 363–5, 367, 385–6
Sport and General, 402
Swedish Travel Bureau, 366
Topical Press, 396
Union-Castle Mail Steamship Company, 351
United States Information Service, 404–5
D. Weatherston, 368
Whitbread and Company Limited, 160